D0821306

PN
1077
.S3
1970

Santayana, George

Three philosophi-
cal poets: Lucre-
tius, Dante, and
Goethe

DATE DUE

DEC 1 1 '78			

COLLEGE OF MARIN LIBRARY
COLLEGE AVENUE
KENTFIELD, CA 94904

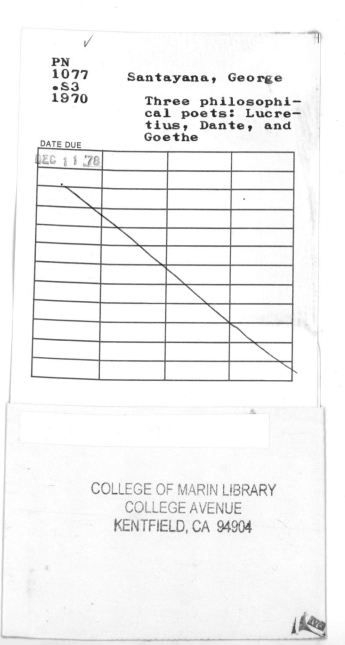

HARVARD STUDIES
IN COMPARATIVE LITERATURE

FOUNDED BY THE GENERAL EDITOR

WILLIAM HENRY SCHOFIELD

PROFESSOR OF COMPARATIVE LITERATURE

IN HARVARD UNIVERSITY

I

THREE PHILOSOPHICAL POETS

LUCRETIUS, DANTE, AND

GOETHE

HARVARD STUDIES IN COMPARATIVE LITERATURE

VOLUME I

THREE
PHILOSOPHICAL POETS

LUCRETIUS, DANTE, AND GOETHE

BY

GEORGE SANTAYANA

FORMERLY PROFESSOR OF PHILOSOPHY IN HARVARD UNIVERSITY

NEW YORK
COOPER SQUARE PUBLISHERS, INC.
1970

Originally Published and Copyright © 1910 by
Harvard University Press
Copyright © Renewed 1938 by George Santayana
Reprinted by Permission of Daniel M. Cory, 1970
Published 1970 by Cooper Square Publishers, Inc.
59 Fourth Avenue, New York, N. Y. 10003
International Standard Book No. 0-8154-0361-5
Library of Congress Catalog Card No. 74-134467

Printed in the United States of America

PREFACE

THE present volume is composed, with a few additions, of six lectures read at Columbia University in February, 1910, and repeated in April of the same year, at the University of Wisconsin. These lectures, in turn, were based on a regular course which I had been giving for some time at Harvard College. Though produced under such learned auspices, my book can make no great claims to learning. It contains the impressions of an amateur, the appreciations of an ordinary reader, concerning three great writers, two of whom at least might furnish matter enough for the studies of a lifetime, and actually have academies, libraries, and university chairs especially consecrated to their memory. I am no specialist in the study of Lucretius; I am not a Dante scholar nor a Goethe scholar. I can report no facts and propose no hypotheses about these men which are not at hand in their familiar works, or in well-known commentaries upon them. My excuse for writing about them, notwithstanding, is merely the human excuse which every new poet has for writing about the spring. They have attracted me; they have moved me to reflection; they have revealed to me certain aspects of nature and of philosophy which I am prompted by mere sincerity to express, if anybody seems interested or willing to listen. What I can offer the benevolent reader, therefore, is no learned investigation. It is only a piece of literary criticism, together with a first broad lesson in the history of philosophy—and, perhaps, in philosophy itself.

G. S.

Harvard College
June, 1910

CONTENTS

I

INTRODUCTION

Lucretius, Dante, and Goethe sum up the chief phases of European philosophy,—naturalism, supernaturalism, and romanticism : Ideal relation between philosophy and poetry.

II

LUCRETIUS

Development of Greek cosmology : Democritus : Epicurean moral sentiment : Changes inspired by it in the system of Democritus : Accidental alliance of materialism with hedonism : Imaginative value of naturalism : The Lucretian Venus, or the propitious movement in nature : The Lucretian Mars, or the destructive movement : Preponderant melancholy, and the reason for it : Materiality of the soul : The fear of death and the fear of life : Lucretius a true poet of nature : Comparison with Shelley and Wordsworth : Things he might have added consistently : Indefeasible worth of his insight and sentiment.

III

DANTE

Character of Platonism : Its cosmology a parable : Combination of this with Hebraic philosophy of history : Theory of the Papacy and the Empire adopted by Dante : His judgement on Florence : Dante as a lyric poet : Beatrice the woman, the symbol, and the reality : Love, magic, and symbolism constitutive principles of Dante's universe : Idea of the Divine Comedy : The scheme of virtues and vices : Retributive theory of rewards and punishments : Esoteric view of this, which makes even punishment intrinsic to the sins : Examples : Dantesque cosmography : The genius of the poet : His universal scope : His triumphant execution of the Comedy : His defects, in spite of which he remains the type of a supreme poet.

CONTENTS

INTRODUCTION

INTRODUCTION

THE sole advantage in possessing great works of literature lies in what they can help us to become. In themselves, as feats performed by their authors, they would have forfeited none of their truth or greatness if they had perished before our day. We can neither take away nor add to their past value or inherent dignity. It is only they, in so far as they are appropriate food and not poison for us, that can add to the present value and dignity of our minds. Foreign classics have to be retranslated and reinterpreted for each generation, to render their old naturalness in a natural way, and keep their perennial humanity living and capable of assimilation. Even native classics have to be reapprehended by every reader. It is this continual digestion of the substance supplied by the past that alone renders the insights of the past still potent in the present and for the future. Living criticism, genuine appreciation, is the interest we draw from year to year on the unrecoverable capital of human genius.

Regarded from this point of view, as substances to be digested, the poetic remains of Lucretius, Dante, and Goethe (though it is his *Faust* only that I shall speak of) afford rather a varied feast. In their doctrine and genius they may seem to be too much opposed to be at all convergent or combinable in their wisdom. Some, who know and care for one, perhaps, of these poets, may be disposed to doubt whether they have anything vital to learn from the other two. Yet it is as a pupil—I hope a discriminating pupil—of each in turn that I mean to speak; and I venture to maintain that in what makes them great they are compatible; that without any vagueness or doubleness in one's criterion of taste one may admire enthusiastically the poetry of each in turn; and that one may accept the essential philosophy, the positive intuition, of each, without lack of definition or system in one's own thinking.

Indeed, the diversity of these three poets passes, if I may use the Hegelian dialect, into a unity of a higher kind. Each is typical of an age. Taken together they sum up all European philosophy. Lucretius adopts the most radical and the most correct of those cosmological systems which the genius of early Greece had devised. He sees the world to be one great edifice, one great machine, all its parts reacting upon one another, and growing out of one another in obedience to a general pervasive process or life. His poem describes the nature, that is, the birth and composition, of all things. It shows how they are compounded out of elements, and how these elements, which he thinks are atoms in perpetual motion, are being constantly redistributed, so that old things perish and new things arise. Into this view of the world he fits a view of human life as it ought to be led under such conditions. His materialism is completed by an aspiration towards freedom and quietness of spirit. Allowed to look once upon the wonderful spectacle, which is to repeat itself in the world for ever, we should look and admire, for to-morrow we die; we should eat, drink, and be merry, but moderately and with much art, lest we die miserably, and die to-day.

This is one complete system of philosophy,—materialism in natural science, humanism in ethics. Such was the gist of all Greek philosophy before Socrates, of that philosophy which was truly Hellenic and corresponded with the movement which produced Greek manners, Greek government, and Greek art—a movement towards simplicity, autonomy, and reasonableness in everything, from dress to religion. Such is the gist also of what may be called the philosophy of the Renaissance, the reassertion of science and liberty in the modern world, by Bacon, by Spinoza, by the whole contemporary school that looks to science for its view of the facts, and to the happiness of men on earth for its ideal. This system is called naturalism; and of this Lucretius is the unrivalled poet.

Skip a thousand years and more, and a contrasting spectacle is before us. All minds, all institutions, are dominated by a religion that represents the soul as a pilgrim upon earth; the world is fallen and subject to the devil; pain and poverty are considered normal, happiness impossible here and to be hoped for only in a future life, provided the snares and pleasures of the present life have not entrapped us. Meantime a sort of Jacob's ladder stretches from the stone on which the wayfarer lays his head into the heaven he hopes for; and the angels he sees ascending and descending upon it are beautiful stories, wonderful theories, and comforting rites. Through these he partakes, even on earth, of what will be his heavenly existence. He partly understands his destiny; his own history and that of the world are transfigured before him and, without ceasing to be sad, become beautiful. The raptures of a perfect conformity with the will of God, and of union with Him, overtake him in his prayers. This is supernaturalism, a system represented in Christendom chiefly by the Catholic Church, but adopted also by the later pagans, and widespread in Asia from remote antiquity down to the present time. Little as the momentary temper of Europe and America may now incline to such a view, it is always possible for the individual, or for the race, to return to it. Its sources are in the solitude of the spirit and in the disparity, or the opposition, between what the spirit feels it is fitted to do, and what, in this world, it is con-

demned to waste itself upon. The unmatched poet
of this supernaturalism is Dante.

Skip again some five hundred years, and there is
another change of scene. The Teutonic races that
had previously conquered Europe have begun to
dominate and understand themselves. They have become Protestants, or protesters against the Roman
world. An infinite fountain of life seems to be unlocked within their bosom. They turn successively
to the Bible, to learning, to patriotism, to industry,
for new objects to love and fresh worlds to con-
quer; but they have too much vitality, or too little
maturity, to rest in any of these things. A demon
drives them on; and this demon, divine and immortal in its apparent waywardness, is their inmost self.
It is their insatiable will, their radical courage. Nay,
though this be a hard saying to the uninitiated, their
will is the creator of all those objects by which it is
sometimes amused, and sometimes baffled, but never
tamed. Their will summons all opportunities and
dangers out of nothing to feed its appetite for action;
and in that ideal function lies their sole reality. Once
attained, things are transcended. Like the episodes
of a spent dream, they are to be smiled at and forgotten; the spirit that feigned and discarded them
remains always strong and undefiled; it aches for
new conquests over new fictions. This is romanticism. It is an attitude often found in English poetry,

and characteristic of German philosophy. It was adopted by Emerson and ought to be sympathetic to Americans; for it expresses the self-trust of world-building youth, and mystical faith in will and action. The greatest monument to this romanticism is Goethe's *Faust*.

Can it be an accident that the most adequate and probably the most lasting exposition of these three schools of philosophy should have been made by poets? Are poets, at heart, in search of a philosophy? Or is philosophy, in the end, nothing but poetry? Let us consider the situation.

If we think of philosophy as an investigation into truth, or as reasoning upon truths supposed to be discovered, there is nothing in philosophy akin to poetry. There is nothing poetic about the works of Epicurus, or St. Thomas Aquinas, or Kant; they are leafless forests. In Lucretius and in Dante themselves we find passages where nothing is poetical except the metre, or some incidental ornament. In such passages the form of poetry is thrown over the substance of prose, as Lucretius himself confesses where he says: "As when physicians would contrive to administer loathsome wormwood to little boys they first moisten the rim of the cup round about with sweet and golden honey, that the children's unsuspecting youth may be beguiled—to the lips, but no further—while they drink down the bitter potion,

by deception not betrayed, but rather by that stratagem made whole and restored; . . . so I have willed
to set forth our doctrine before thee in sweet-sound-
ing Pierian song, and to smear it, as it were, with
the Muses' honey."[1]

But poetry cannot be spread upon things like
butter; it must play upon them like light, and be
the medium through which we see them. Lucretius
does himself an injustice. If his philosophy had been
wormwood to him, he could not have said, as he does
just before this passage: "Like a sharp blow of the
thyrsus, a great hope of praise vibrates through my
heart and fills my breast with tender love of the
Muses, whereby now, instinct with flowering fancy,
I traverse pathless haunts of the Pierides, by no
man's foot trodden before. It is joy to reach undefiled fountains and quaff; it is joy to gather fresh
flowers and weave a matchless crown for my head
of those bays with which never yet the Muses veiled
the brow of any man; first, in that I teach sublime

---

[1] Lucretius, I. 936–47:

> Veluti pueris absinthia tetra medentes
> Cum dare conantur, prius oras pocula circum
> Contingunt mellis dulci flavoque liquore,
> Ut puerorum aetas improvida ludificetur
> Labrorum tenus, interea perpotet amarum
> Absinthi laticem, deceptaque non capiatur,
> Sed potius tali pacto recreata valescat:
> Sic ego nunc . . . volui tibi suaviloquenti
> Carmine Pierio rationem exponere nostram,
> Et quasi musaeo dulci contingere melle.

truths and come to free the soul from the strangling knots of superstition; then, in that on so dark a theme I pour forth so clear a song, suffusing all with poetic beauty, . . . if haply by such means I might keep thy mind intent upon my verses, until thine eye fathoms the whole structure of nature, and the fixed form that makes it beautiful."[1]

Here, I think, we have the solution to our doubt. The reasonings and investigations of philosophy are arduous, and if poetry is to be linked with them, it can be artificially only, and with a bad grace. But the vision of philosophy is sublime. The order it reveals in the world is something beautiful, tragic, sympathetic to the mind, and just what every poet, on a small or on a large scale, is always trying to catch.

In philosophy itself investigation and reasoning are only preparatory and servile parts, means to an

---

[1] Lucretius, I. 922–34, 948–50:

Acri

Percussit thyrso laudis spes magna meum cor
Et simul incussit suavem mi in pectus amorem
Musarum, quo nunc instinctus mente vigenti
Avia Pieridum peragro loca nullius ante
Trita solo: iuvat integros accedere fontes,
Atque haurire; iuvatque novos decerpere flores,
Insignemque meo capiti petere inde coronam,
Unde prius nulli velarint tempora musae.
Primum, quod magnis doceo de rebus, et artis
Religionum animum nodis exsolvere pergo:
Deinde, quod obscura de re tam lucida pango
Carmina, musaeo contingens cuncta lepore. . . .
Si tibi forte animum tali ratione tenere
Versibus in nostris possem, dum perspicis omnem
Naturam rerum, qua constet compta figura.

end. They terminate in insight, or what in the noblest sense of the word may be called *theory*, θεωρία,— a steady contemplation of all things in their order and worth. Such contemplation is imaginative. No one can reach it who has not enlarged his mind and tamed his heart. A philosopher who attains it is, for the moment, a poet; and a poet who turns his practised and passionate imagination on the order of all things, or on anything in the light of the whole, is for that moment a philosopher.

Nevertheless, even if we grant that the philosopher, in his best moments, is a poet, we may suspect that the poet has his worst moments when he tries to be a philosopher, or rather, when he succeeds in being one. Philosophy is something reasoned and heavy; poetry something winged, flashing, inspired. Take almost any longish poem, and the parts of it are better than the whole. A poet is able to put together a few words, a cadence or two, a single interesting image. He renders in that way some moment of comparatively high tension, of comparatively keen sentiment. But at the next moment the tension is relaxed, the sentiment has faded, and what succeeds is usually incongruous with what went before, or at least inferior. The thought drifts away from what it had started to be. It is lost in the sands of versification. As man is now constituted, to be brief is almost a condition of being inspired.

Shall we say, then,—and I now broach an idea by which I set some store,—that poetry is essentially short-winded, that what is poetic is necessarily intermittent in the writings of poets, that only the fleeting moment, the mood, the episode, can be rapturously felt, or rapturously rendered, while life as a whole, history, character, and destiny are objects unfit for imagination to dwell on, and repellent to poetic art? I cannot think so. If it be a fact, as it often is, that we find little things pleasing and great things arid and formless, and if we are better poets in a line than in an epic, that is simply due to lack of faculty on our part, lack of imagination and memory, and above all to lack of discipline.

This might be shown, I think, by psychological analysis, if we cared to rely on something so abstract and so debatable. For in what does the short-winded poet himself excel the common unimaginative person who talks or who stares? Is it that he thinks even less? Rather, I suppose, in that he feels more; in that his moment of intuition, though fleeting, has a vision, a scope, a symbolic something about it that renders it deep and expressive. Intensity, even momentary intensity, if it can be expressed at all, comports fullness and suggestion compressed into that intense moment. Yes, everything that comes to us at all must come to us at some time or other. It is always the fleeting moment in which we live. To this fleeting moment the philosopher, as well as the poet, is actually confined. Each must enrich it with his endless vistas, vistas necessarily focused, if they are to be disclosed at all, in the eye of the observer, here and now. What makes the difference between a moment of poetic insight and a vulgar moment is that the passions of the poetic moment have more perspective. Even the short-winded poet selects his words so that they have a magic momentum in them which carries us, we know not how, to mountain-tops of intuition. Is not the poetic quality of phrases and images due to their concentrating and liberating the confused promptings left in us by a long experience? When we feel the poetic thrill, is it not that we find sweep in the concise and depth in the clear, as we might find all the lights of the sea in the water of a jewel? And what is a philosophic thought but such an epitome?

If a short passage is poetical because it is pregnant with suggestion of a few things, which stretches our attention and makes us rapt and serious, how much more poetical ought a vision to be which was pregnant with all we care for? Focus a little experience, give some scope and depth to your feeling, and it grows imaginative; give it more scope and more depth, focus all experience within it, make it a philosopher's vision of the world, and it will grow imaginative in a superlative degree, and be supremely poetical. The difficulty, after having the experience to symbolize, lies only in having enough imagination to hold and suspend it in a thought; and further to give this thought such verbal expression that others may be able to decipher it, and to be stirred by it as by a wind of suggestion sweeping the whole forest of their memories.

Poetry, then, is not poetical for being short-winded or incidental, but, on the contrary, for being comprehensive and having range. If too much matter renders it heavy, that is the fault of the poet's weak intellect, not of the outstretched world. A quicker eye, a more synthetic imagination, might grasp a larger subject with the same ease. The picture that would render this larger subject would not be flatter and feebler for its extent, but, on the contrary, deeper and stronger, since it would possess as much unity as the little one with greater volume. As in a supreme dramatic crisis all our life seems to be focused in the present, and used in colouring our consciousness and shaping our decisions, so for each philosophic poet the whole world of man is gathered together; and he is never so much a poet as when, in a single cry, he summons all that has affinity to him in the universe, and salutes his ultimate destiny. It is the acme of life to understand life. The height of poetry is to speak the language of the gods.

But enough of psychological analysis and of reasoning in the void. Three historical illustrations will prove my point more clearly and more conclusively.

LUCRETIUS

LUCRETIUS

THERE is perhaps no important poem the antecedents of which can be traced so exhaustively as can those of the work of Lucretius, *De Rerum Natura.* These antecedents, however, do not lie in the poet himself. If they did, we should not be able to trace them, since we know nothing, or next to nothing, about Lucretius the man. In a chronicon, compiled by St. Jerome largely out of Suetonius, in which miscellaneous events are noted which occurred in each successive year, we read for the year 94 B.C.: "Titus Lucretius, poet, is born. After a love-philtre had turned him mad, and he had written, in the intervals of his insanity, several books which Cicero revised, he killed himself by his own hand in the forty-fourth year of his age."

The love-philtre in this report sounds apocryphal; and the story of the madness and suicide attributes too edifying an end to an atheist and Epicurean not to be suspected. If anything lends colour to the story it is a certain consonance which we may feel between its tragic incidents and the genius of the poet as revealed in his work, where we find a strange scorn of love, a strange vehemence, and a high melancholy. It is by no means incredible that the author of such a poem should have been at some time the slave of a pathological passion, that his vehemence and inspiration should have passed into mania, and that he should have taken his own life. But the untrustworthy authority of St. Jerome cannot assure us whether what he repeats is a tradition founded on fact or an ingenious fiction.

Our ignorance of the life of Lucretius is not, I think, much to be regretted. His work preserves that part of him which he himself would have wished to preserve. Perfect conviction ignores itself, proclaiming the public truth. To reach this no doubt requires a peculiar genius which is called intelligence; for intelligence is quickness in seeing things as they are. But where intelligence is attained, the rest of a man, like the scaffolding to a finished building, becomes irrelevant. We do not wish it to intercept our view of the solid structure, which alone was intended by the artist—if he was building for others, and was not a coxcomb. It is his intellectual vision that the naturalist in particular wishes to hand down to posterity, not the shabby incidents that preceded that vision in his own person. These incidents, even if they were by chance interesting, could not be repeated in us; but the vision into which the thinker poured his faculties, and to which he devoted his vigils, is communicable to us also, and may become a part of ourselves.

Since Lucretius is thus identical for us with his

poem, and is lost in his philosophy, the antecedents
of Lucretius are simply the stages by which his conception of nature first shaped itself in the human
mind. To retrace these stages is easy; some of them
are only too familiar; yet the very triteness of the
subject may blind us to the grandeur and audacity
of the intellectual feat involved. A naturalistic conception of things is a great work of imagination,—
greater, I think, than any dramatic or moral mythology: it is a conception fit to inspire great poetry,
and in the end, perhaps, it will prove the only conception able to inspire it.

We are told of the old Xenophanes that he looked
up into the round heaven and cried, "The All is
One." What is logically a truism may often be,
imaginatively, a great discovery, because no one before may have thought of the obvious analogy which
the truism registers. So, in this case, the unity of all
things is logically an evident, if barren, truth; for
the most disparate and unrelated worlds would still
be a multitude, and so an aggregate, and so, in some
sense, a unity. Yet it was a great imaginative feat
to cast the eye deliberately round the entire horizon,
and to draw mentally the sum of all reality, discov-
ering that reality makes such a sum, and may be
called one; as any stone or animal, though composed
of many parts, is yet called one in common parlance.
It was doubtless some prehistoric man of genius,

long before Xenophanes, who first applied in this way to all things together that notion of unity and wholeness which everybody had gained by observation of things singly, and who first ventured to speak of "the world." To do so is to set the problem for all natural philosophy, and in a certain measure to anticipate the solution of that problem; for it is to ask how things hang together, and to assume that they do hang together in one way or another.

To cry "The All is One," and to perceive that all things are in one landscape and form a system by their juxtaposition, is the rude beginning of wisdom in natural philosophy. But it is easy to go farther, and to see that things form a unity in a far deeper and more mysterious way. One of the first things, for instance, that impresses the poet, the man of feeling and reflection, is that these objects that people the world all pass away, and that the place thereof knows them no more. Yet, when they vanish, nothingness does not succeed; other things arise in their stead. Nature remains always young and whole in spite of death at work everywhere; and what takes the place of what continually disappears is often remarkably like it in character. Universal instability is not incompatible with a great monotony in things; so that while Heraclitus lamented that everything was in flux, Ecclesiastes, who was also entirely convinced of that truth, could lament that there was nothing new under the sun.

This double experience of mutation and recurrence, an experience at once sentimental and scientific, soon brought with it a very great thought, perhaps the greatest thought that mankind has ever hit upon, and which was the chief inspiration of Lucretius. It is that all we observe about us, and ourselves also, may be so many passing forms of a permanent substance. This substance, while remaining the same in quantity and in inward quality, is constantly redistributed; in its redistribution it forms those aggregates which we call things, and which we find constantly disappearing and reappearing. All things are dust, and to dust they return; a dust, however, eternally fertile, and destined to fall perpetually into new, and doubtless beautiful, forms. This notion of substance lends a much greater unity to the outspread world; it persuades us that all things pass into one another, and have a common ground from which they spring successively, and to which they return.

The spectacle of inexorable change, the triumph of time, or whatever we may call it, has always been a favourite theme for lyric and tragic poetry, and for religious meditation. To perceive universal mutation, to feel the vanity of life, has always been the beginning of seriousness. It is the condition for any beautiful, measured, or tender philosophy. Prior to that, everything is barbarous, both in morals and in poetry; for until then mankind has not learned to renounce anything, has not outgrown the instinctive egotism and optimism of the young animal, and has not removed the centre of its being, or of its faith, from the will to the imagination.

To discover substance, then, is a great step in the life of reason, even if substance be conceived quite negatively as a term that serves merely to mark, by contrast, the unsubstantiality, the vanity, of all particular moments and things. That is the way in which Indian poetry and philosophy conceived substance. But the step taken by Greek physics, and by the poetry of Lucretius, passes beyond. Lucretius and the Greeks, in observing universal mutation and the vanity of life, conceived behind appearance a great intelligible process, an evolution in nature. The reality became interesting, as well as the illusion. Physics became scientific, which had previously been merely spectacular.

Here was a much richer theme for the poet and philosopher, who was launched upon the discovery of the ground and secret causes of this gay or melancholy flux. The understanding that enabled him to discover these causes did for the European what no Indian mystic, what no despiser of understanding anywhere, suffers himself to do; namely, to dominate, foretell, and transform this changing show with a virile, practical intelligence. The man who discovers the secret springs of appearances opens to contemplation a second positive world, the workshop and busy depths of nature, where a prodigious mechanism is continually supporting our life, and making ready for it from afar by the most exquisite adjustments. The march of this mechanism, while it produces life and often fosters it, yet as often makes it difficult and condemns it to extinction. This truth, which the conception of natural substance first makes intelligible, justifies the elegies which the poets of illusion and disillusion have always written upon human things. It is a truth with a melancholy side; but being a truth, it satisfies and exalts the rational mind, that craves truth as truth, whether it be sad or comforting, and wishes to pursue a possible, not an impossible, happiness.

So far, Greek science had made out that the world was one, that there was a substance, that this was a physical substance, distributed and moving in space. It was matter. The question remained, What is the precise nature of matter, and how does it produce the appearances we observe? The only answer that concerns us here is that given by Lucretius; an answer he accepted from Epicurus, his master in everything, who in turn had accepted it from Democritus. Now Democritus had made a notable advance over the systems that selected one obvious substance, like water, or collected all the obvious substances, as Anaxagoras had done, and tried to make the world out of them. Democritus thought that the substance of everything ought not to have any of the qualities present in some things and absent in others; it ought to have only the qualities present in all things. It should be *merely* matter. Materiality, according to him, consisted of extension, figure, and solidity; in the thinnest ether, if we looked sharp enough, we should find nothing but particles possessing these properties. All other qualities of things were apparent only, and imputed to them by a convention of the mind. The mind was a born mythologist, and projected its feelings into their causes. Light, colour, taste, warmth, beauty, excellence, were such imputed and conventional qualities; only space and matter were real. But empty space was no less real than matter. Consequently, although the atoms of matter never changed their form, real changes could take place in nature, because their position might change in a real space.

Unlike the useless substance of the Indians, the substance of Democritus could offer a calculable ground for the flux of appearances; for this substance was distributed unequally in the void, and was constantly moving. Every appearance, however fleeting, corresponded to a precise configuration of substance;

it arose with that configuration and perished with it. This substance, accordingly, was physical, not metaphysical. It was no dialectical term, but a scientific anticipation, a prophecy as to what an observer who should be properly equipped would discover in the interior of bodies. Materialism is not a system of metaphysics; it is a speculation in chemistry and physiology, to the effect that, if analysis could go deep enough, it would find that all substance was homogeneous, and that all motion was regular.

Though matter was homogeneous, the forms of the ultimate particles, according to Democritus, were various; and sundry combinations of them constituted the sundry objects in nature. Motion was not, as the vulgar (and Aristotle) supposed, unnatural, and produced magically by some moral cause; it had been eternal and was native to the atoms. On striking, they rebounded; and the mechanical currents or vortices which these contacts occasioned formed a multitude of stellar systems, called worlds, with which infinite space was studded.

Mechanism as to motion, atomism as to structure, materialism as to substance, that is the whole system of Democritus. It is as wonderful in its insight, in its sense for the ideal demands of method and understanding, as it is strange and audacious in its simplicity. Only the most convinced rationalist, the boldest prophet, could embrace it dogmatically; yet time has largely given it the proof. If Democritus could look down upon the present state of science, he would laugh, as he was in the habit of doing, partly at the confirmation we can furnish to portions of his philosophy, and partly at our stupidity that cannot guess the rest.

There are two maxims in Lucretius that suffice, even to this day, to distinguish a thinker who is a naturalist from one who is not. "Nothing," he says, "arises in the body in order that we may use it, but what arises brings forth its use."[1] This is that discarding of final causes on which all progress in science depends. The other maxim runs: "One thing will grow plain when compared with another: and blind night shall not obliterate the path for thee, before thou hast thoroughly scanned the ultimate things of nature; so much will things throw light on things."[2] Nature is her own standard; and if she seems to us unnatural, there is no hope for our minds.

The ethics of Democritus, in so far as we may judge from scanty evidence, were merely descriptive or satirical. He was an aristocratic observer, a scorner of fools. Nature was laughing at us all; the wise man

---

[1] Lucretius, iv. 834, 835:
　　　Nil . . . natumst in corpore, ut uti
　　　Possemus, sed quod natumst id procreat usum.

[2] Ibid., i. 1115-18:
　　　Alid ex alio clarescet, nec tibi caeca
　　　Nox iter eripiet, quin ultima naturai
　　　Pervideas: ita res accendent lumina rebus.

considered his fate and, by knowing it, raised himself in a measure above it. All living things pursued
the greatest happiness they could see their way to;
but they were marvellously short-sighted; and the
business of the philosopher was to foresee and pursue the greatest happiness that was really possible.
This, in so rough a world, was to be found chiefly in
abstention and retrenchment. If you asked for little,
it was more probable that the event would not dis-
appoint you. It was important not to be a fool, but
it was very hard.

The system of Democritus was adopted by Epicurus, but not because Epicurus had any keenness of
scientific vision. On the contrary, Epicurus, the Her-
bert Spencer of antiquity, was in his natural philosophy an encyclopaedia of second-hand knowledge.
Prolix and minute, vague and inconsistent, he gathered his scientific miscellany with an eye fixed not
on nature, but on the exigencies of an inward faith,
—a faith accepted on moral grounds, deemed necessary to salvation, and defended at all costs, with any
available weapon. It is instructive that materialism
should have been adopted at that juncture on the
same irrelevant moral grounds on which it has usually been rejected.

Epicurus, strange as it may sound to those who
have heard, with horror or envy, of wallowing in his
sty, Epicurus was a saint. The ways of the world

filled him with dismay. The Athens of his time, which some of us would give our eyes to see, retained all its splendour amid its political decay; but nothing there interested or pleased Epicurus. Theatres, porches, gymnasiums, and above all the agora, reeked, to his sense, with vanity and folly. Retired in his private garden, with a few friends and disciples, he sought the ways of peace; he lived abstemiously; he spoke gently; he gave alms to the poor; he preached against wealth, against ambition, against passion. He defended free-will because he wished to exercise it in withdrawing from the world, and in not swimming with the current. He denied the supernatural, since belief in it would have a disquieting influence on the mind, and render too many things compulsory and momentous. There was no future life: the art of living wisely must not be distorted by such wild imaginings.

All things happened in due course of nature; the gods were too remote and too happy, secluded like good Epicureans, to meddle with earthly things. Nothing ruffled what Wordsworth calls their "voluptuous unconcern." Nevertheless, it was pleasant to frequent their temples. There, as in the spaces where they dwelt between the worlds, the gods were silent and beautiful, and wore the human form. Their statues, when an unhappy man gazed at them, reminded him of happiness; he was refreshed and weaned for a moment from the senseless tumult of human affairs. From those groves and hallowed sanctuaries the philosopher returned to his garden strengthened in his wisdom, happier in his isolation, more friendly and more indifferent to all the world. Thus the life of Epicurus, as St. Jerome bears witness, was "full of herbs, fruits, and abstinences." There was a hush in it, as of bereavement. His was a philosophy of the decadence, a philosophy of negation, and of flight from the world.

Although science for its own sake could not interest so monkish a nature, yet science might be useful in buttressing the faith, or in removing objections to it. Epicurus therefore departed from the reserve of Socrates, and looked for a natural philosophy that might support his ethics. Of all the systems extant—and they were legion—he found that of Democritus the most helpful and edifying. Better than any other it would persuade men to renounce the madness that must be renounced and to enjoy the pleasures that may be enjoyed. But, since it was adopted on these external and pragmatic grounds, the system of Democritus did not need to be adopted entire. In fact, one change at least was imperative. The motion of the atoms must not be wholly regular and mechanical. Chance must be admitted, that Fate might be removed. Fate was a terrifying notion. It was spoken of by the people with superstitious unction. Chance was something humbler, more congenial to the man in the street. If only the atoms were allowed to deflect a little now and then from their courses, the future might remain unpredictable, and free-will might be saved. Therefore, Epicurus decreed that the atoms deflected, and fantastic arguments were added to show that this intrusion of chance would aid in the organization of nature; for the declension of the atoms, as it is called, would explain how the original parallel downpour of them might have yielded to vortices, and so to organized bodies. Let us pass on.

Materialism, like any system of natural philosophy, carries with it no commandments and no advice. It merely describes the world, including the aspirations and consciences of mortals, and refers all to a material ground. The materialist, being a man, will not fail to have preferences, and even a conscience, of his own; but his precepts and policy will express, not the logical implications of his science, but his human instincts, as inheritance and experience may have shaped them. Any system of ethics might accordingly coexist with materialism; for if materialism declares certain things (like immortality) to be impossible, it cannot declare them to be undesirable. Nevertheless, it is not likely that a man so constituted as to embrace materialism will be so constituted as to pursue things which he considers unattainable. There is therefore a psychological, though no logical, bond between materialism and a homely morality.

The materialist is primarily an observer; and he will probably be such in ethics also; that is, he will have no ethics, except the emotion produced upon him by the march of the world. If he is an *esprit fort* and really disinterested, he will love life; as we all love perfect vitality, or what strikes us as such, in gulls and porpoises. This, I think, is the ethical sentiment psychologically consonant with a vigorous materialism: sympathy with the movement of things, interest in the rising wave, delight at the foam it bursts into, before it sinks again. Nature does not distinguish the better from the worse, but the lover of nature does. He calls better what, being analogous to his own life, enhances his vitality and probably possesses some vitality of its own. This is the ethical feeling of Spinoza, the greatest of modern naturalists in philosophy; and we shall see how Lucretius, in spite of his fidelity to the ascetic Epicurus, is carried by his poetic ecstasy in the same direction.

But mark the crux of this union: the materialist will love the life of nature when he loves his own life; but if he should hate his own life, how should the life of nature please him? Now Epicurus, for the most part, hated life. His moral system, called he-donism, recommends that sort of pleasure which has no excitement and no risk about it. This ideal is modest, and even chaste, but it is not vital. Epicurus was remarkable for his mercy, his friendliness, his utter horror of war, of sacrifice, of suffering. These are not sentiments that a genuine naturalist would be apt to share. Pity and repentance, Spinoza said, were vain and evil; what increased a man's power and his joy increased his goodness also. The naturalist will believe in a certain hardness, as Nietzsche did; he will incline to a certain scorn, as the laughter of Democritus was scornful. He will not count too scrupulously the cost of what he achieves; he will be an imperialist, rapt in the joy of achieving something. In a word, the moral hue of materialism in a formative age, or in an aggressive mind, would be aristocratic and imaginative; but in a decadent age, or in a soul that is renouncing everything, it would be, as in Epicurus, humanitarian and timidly sensual.

We have now before us the antecedents and components of Lucretius' poem on nature. There remains the genius of the poet himself. The greatest thing about this genius is its power of losing itself in its object, its impersonality. We seem to be reading not the poetry of a poet about things, but the poetry of things themselves. That things have their poetry, not because of what we make them symbols of, but because of their own movement and life, is what Lucretius proves once for all to mankind.

Of course, the poetry we see in nature is due to the emotion the spectacle produces in us; the life of nature might be as romantic and sublime as it chose, it would be dust and ashes to us if there were nothing sublime and romantic in ourselves to be stirred by it to sympathy. But our emotion may be ingenuous; it may be concerned with what nature really is and does, has been and will do for ever. It need not arise from a selfish preoccupation with what these immense realities involve for our own persons or may be used to suggest to our self-indulgent fancy. No, the poetry of nature may be discerned merely by the power of intuition which it awakens and the understanding which it employs. These faculties, more, I should say, than our moodiness or stuffy dreams, draw taut the strings of the soul, and bring out her full vitality and music. Naturalism is a philosophy of observation, and of an imagination that extends the observable; all the sights and sounds of nature enter into it, and lend it their directness, pungency, and coercive stress. At the same time, naturalism is an intellectual philosophy; it divines substance behind appearance, continuity behind change, law behind fortune. It therefore attaches all those sights and sounds to a hidden background that connects and explains them. So understood, nature has depth as well as surface, force and necessity as well as sensuous variety. Before the sublimity of this insight, all forms of the pathetic fallacy seem cheap and artificial. Mythology, that to a childish mind is the only possible poetry, sounds like bad rhetoric in comparison. The naturalistic poet abandons fairy land, because he has discovered nature, history, the actual passions of man. His imagination has reached maturity; its pleasure is to dominate, not to play.

Poetic dominion over things as they are is seen best in Shakespeare for the ways of men, and in Lucretius for the ways of nature. Unapproachably vivid, relentless, direct in detail, he is unflinchingly grand and serious in his grouping of the facts. It is the truth that absorbs him and carries him along. He wishes us to be convinced and sobered by the fact, by the overwhelming evidence of thing after thing, raining down upon us, all bearing witness with one voice to the nature of the world.

Suppose, however,—and it is a tenable supposition,—that Lucretius is quite wrong in his science, and that there is no space, no substance, and no nature. His poem would then lose its pertinence to our lives and personal convictions; it would not lose its imaginative grandeur. We could still conceive a world composed as he describes. Fancy what emotions those who lived in such a world would have felt on the day when a Democritus or a Lucretius revealed to them their actual situation. How great the blindness or the madness dissipated, and how wonderful the vision gained! How clear the future, how intelligible the past, how marvellous the swarming atoms, in their unintentional, perpetual fertility! What the sky is to our eyes on a starry night, that every nook and cranny of nature would resemble, with here and there the tentative smile of life playing about those constellations. Surely that universe, for those who lived in it, would have had its poetry. It would have been the poetry of naturalism. Lucretius, thinking he lived in such a world, heard the music of it, and wrote it down.

And yet, when he set himself to make his poem out of the system of Epicurus, the greatness of that task seems to have overwhelmed him. He was to unfold for the first time, in sonorous but unwieldy Latin, the birth and nature of all things, as Greek subtlety had discerned them. He was to dispel superstition, to refute antagonists, to lay the sure foundations of science and of wisdom, to summon mankind compellingly from its cruel passions and follies to a life of simplicity and peace. He was himself combative and distracted enough — as it is often our troubles, more than our attainments, that determine our ideals. Yet in heralding the advent of human happiness, and in painting that of the gods, he was to attain his own, soaring upon the strong wings of his hexameters into an ecstasy of contemplation and enthusiasm. When it is so great an emotion to read these verses, what must it have been to compose them? Yet could he succeed? Could such great things fall to his lot? Yes, they might, if only the creative forces of nature, always infinite and always at hand, could pass into his brain and into his spirit; if only the seeds of corruption and madness, which were always coursing through the air, could be blown back for a moment; and if the din of civil conflicts could be suspended while he thought and wrote. To a fortunate conjunction of atoms, a child owes his first being. To a propitious season and atmosphere, a poet owes his inspiration and his success. Conscious that his undertaking hangs upon these chance conjunctions, Lucretius begins by invoking the powers he is about to describe, that they may give him breath and genius enough to describe them. And at once these powers send him a happy inspiration, perhaps a happy reminiscence of Empedocles. There are two great perspectives which the moralist may distinguish in the universal drift of atoms, — a creative movement, producing what the moralist values, and a destructive movement, abolishing the same. Lucretius knows very well that this distinction is moral only, or as people now say, subjective. No one else has pointed out so often and so clearly as he that nothing arises in this world not helped to life by the death of some other thing;[1] so that the destructive movement creates and the creative movement destroys. Yet from the point of view of any particular life or interest, the distinction between a creative force and a destructive force is real and all-important. To make it is not to deny the mechanical structure of nature, but only to show how this mechanical structure is fruitful morally, how the outlying parts of it are friendly or hostile to me or to you, its local and living products.

This double colouring of things is supremely interesting to the philosopher; so much so that before his physical science has reached the mechanical stage, he will doubtless regard the double aspect which things present to him as a dual principle in these things themselves. So Empedocles had spoken of Love and Strife as two forces which respectively gathered and disrupted the elements, so as to carry on between them the Penelope's labour of the world, the one perpetually weaving fresh forms of life, and the other perpetually undoing them.[2]

It needed but a slight concession to traditional rhetoric in order to exchange these names, Love and

---

[1] Lucretius, I. 264, 265:

> Alid ex alio reficit natura, nec ullam
> Rem gigni patitur, nisi morte adiuta aliena.

[2] An excellent expression of this view is put by Plato into the mouth of the physician Eryximachus in the *Symposium*, pp. 186–88.

Strife, which designated divine powers in Empedocles, into the names of Venus and Mars, which designated the same influences in Roman mythology. The
Mars and Venus of Lucretius are not moral forces,
incompatible with the mechanism of atoms; they are
this mechanism itself, in so far as it now produces
and now destroys life, or any precious enterprise,
like this of Lucretius in composing his saving poem.
Mars and Venus, linked in each other's arms, rule
the universe together; nothing arises save by the
death of some other thing. Yet when what arises is
happier in itself, or more congenial to us, than what
is destroyed, the poet says that Venus prevails, that
she woos her captive lover to suspend his unprofit-
able raging. At such times it is spring on earth; the
storms recede (I paraphrase the opening passage),[1]
the fields are covered with flowers, the sunshine
floods the serene sky, and all the tribes of animals
feel the mighty impulse of Venus in their hearts.

[1] Lucretius, I. 1-13:

> Æneadum genetrix, hominum divomque voluptas,
> Alma Venus, caeli subter labentia signa
> Quae mare navigerum, quae terras frugiferentis
> Concelebras ; per te quoniam genus omne animantum
> Concipitur, visitque exortum lumina solis :
> Te, dea, te fugiunt venti, te nubila caeli,
> Adventumque tuum : tibi suaves daedala tellus
> Submittit flores ; tibi rident aequora ponti,
> Placatumque nitet diffuso lumine caelum.
> Nam simul ac species patefactast verna diei,
> Et reserata viget genitabilis aura favoni ;
> Aëriae primum volucres te, diva, tuumque
> Significant initum, perculsae corda tua vi.

The corn ripens in the plains, and even the sea bears in safety the fleets that traverse it.

Not least, however, of these works of Venus is the Roman people. Never was the formative power of nature better illustrated than in the vitality of this race, which conquered so many other races, or than in its assimilative power, which civilized and pacified them. Legend had made Venus the mother of Aeneas, and Aeneas the progenitor of the Romans. Lucretius seizes on this happy accident and identifies the Venus of fable with the true Venus, the propitious power in all nature, of which Rome was indeed a crowning work. But the poet's work, also, if it is to be accomplished worthily, must look to the same propitious movement for its happy issue and for its power to persuade. Venus must be the patron of his art and philosophy. She must keep Memmius from the wars, that he may read, and be weaned from frivolous ambitions; and she must stop the tumult of constant sedition, that Lucretius may lend his undivided mind to the precepts of Epicurus, and his whole heart to a sublime friendship, which prompts him to devote to intense study all the watches of the starry night, plotting the course of each invisible atom, and mounting almost to the seat of the gods.[1]

1 Lucretius, I. 24, 28–30, 41–43, 140–44:

> Te sociam studeo scribendis versibus esse. . . .
> Quo magis aeternum da dictis, diva, leporem:

This impersonation in the figure of Venus of whatever makes for life would not be legitimate—it would really contradict a mechanical view of nature—if it were not balanced by a figure representing the opposite tendency, the no less universal tendency towards death.

The Mars of the opening passage, subdued for a moment by the blandishments of love, is raging in all the rest of the poem in his irrepressible fury. These are the two sides of every transmutation, that in creating, one thing destroys another; and this transmutation being perpetual,—nothing being durable except the void, the atoms, and their motion,—it follows that the tendency towards death is, for any particular thing, the final and victorious tendency. The names of Venus and Mars, not being essential to the poet's thought, are allowed to drop out, and the actual processes they stand for are described nakedly; yet, if the poem had ever been finished, and Lucretius had wished to make the end chime with the beginning, and represent, as it were, one great

Effice, ut interea fera moenera militiai
Per maria ac terras omnes sopita quiescant. . . .
Nam neque nos agere hoc patriai tempore iniquo
Possumus aequo animo, nec Memmi clara propago
Talibus in rebus communi desse saluti . . .
Sed tua me virtus tamen, et sperata voluptas
Suavis amicitiae, quemvis sufferre laborem
Suadet, et inducit noctes vigilare serenas,
Quaerentem, dictis quibus et quo carmine demum
Clara tuae possim praepandere lumina menti.

cycle of the world, it is conceivable that he might have placed at the close a mythical passage to match that at the beginning; and we might have seen Mars aroused from his luxurious lethargy, reasserting his immortal nature, and rushing, firebrand in hand, from the palace of love to spread destruction throughout the universe, till all things should burn fiercely, and be consumed together. Yet not quite all; for the goddess herself would remain, more divine and desirable than ever in her averted beauty. Instinctively into her bosom the God of War would sink again, when weary and drunk with slaughter; and a new world would arise from the scattered atoms of the old.

These endless revolutions, taken in themselves, exactly balance; and I am not sure that, impartially considered, it is any sadder that new worlds should arise than that this world should always continue. Besides, nature cannot take from us more than she has given, and it would be captious and thankless in us to think of her as destructive only, or destructive essentially, after the unspeculative fashion of modern pessimists. She destroys to create, and creates to destroy, her interest (if we may express it so) being not in particular things, nor in their continuance, but solely in the movement that underlies them, in the flux of substance beneath. Life, however, belongs to form, and not to matter; or in the language of

Lucretius, life is an *eventum*, a redundant ideal product or incidental aspect, involved in the equilibration of matter; as the throw of sixes is an *eventum*, a redundant ideal product or incidental aspect, occasionally involved in shaking a dice-box. Yet, as this throw makes the acme and best possible issue of a game of dice, so life is the acme and best possible issue of the dance of atoms; and it is from the point of view of this *eventum* that the whole process is viewed by us, and is judged. Not until that happy chance has taken place, do we exist morally, or can we reflect or judge at all. The philosopher is at the top of the wave, he is the foam in the rolling tempest; and as the wave must have risen before he bursts into being, all that he lives to witness is the fall of the wave. The decadence of all he lives by is the only prospect before him; his whole philosophy must be a prophecy of death. Of the life that may come after, when the atoms come together again, he can imagine nothing; the life he knows and shares, all that is life to him, is waning and almost spent.

Therefore Lucretius, who is nothing if not honest, is possessed by a profound melancholy. Vigorous and throbbing as are his pictures of spring, of love, of ambition, of budding culture, of intellectual victory, they pale before the vivid strokes with which he paints the approach of death—fatigue of the will, lassitude in pleasure, corruption and disintegration in society, the soil exhausted, the wild animals tamed or exterminated, poverty, pestilence, and famine at hand; and for the individual, almost at once, the final dissipation of the atoms of his soul, escaping from a relaxed body, to mingle and lose themselves in the universal flaw. Nothing comes out of nothing, nothing falls back into nothing, if we consider substance; but everything comes from nothing and falls back into nothing if we consider things—the objects of love and of experience. Time can make no impression on the void or on the atoms; nay, time is itself an *eventum* created by the motion of atoms in the void; but the triumph of time is absolute over persons, and nations, and worlds.[1]

In treating of the soul and of immortality Lucretius is an imperfect psychologist and an arbitrary moralist. His zeal to prove that the soul is mortal is inspired by the wish to dispel all fear of future punishments, and so to liberate the mind for the calm and tepid enjoyment of this world. There is some-

---

[1] Lucretius, II. 1139–41, 1148–49, 1164–74:

> Omnia debet enim cibus integrare novando,
> Et fulcire cibus, cibus omnia sustentare.
> Nequidquam, . . .
> Sic igitur magni quoque circum moenia mundi
> Expugnata dabunt labem putrisque ruinas. . . .
> Iamque caput quassans grandis suspirat arator
> Crebrius incassum manuum cecidisse laborem:
> Et cum tempora temporibus praesentia confert
> Praeteritis, laudat fortunas saepe parentis, . . .
> Nec tenet, omnia paulatim tabescere et ire
> Ad capulum, spatio aetatis defessa vetusto.

thing to be gained in this direction, undoubtedly, especially if tales about divine vengeance to come are used to sanction irrational practices, and to prevent poor people from improving their lot. At the same time, it is hardly fair to assume that hell is the only prospect which immortality could possibly open to any of us; and it is also unfair not to observe that the punishments which religious fables threaten the dead with are, for the most part, symbols for the actual degradation which evil-doing brings upon the living; so that the fear of hell is not more deterrent or repressive than experience of life would be if it were clearly brought before the mind.

There is another element in this polemic against immortality which, while highly interesting and characteristic of a decadent age, betrays a very one-sided and, at bottom, untenable ideal. This element is the fear of life. Epicurus had been a pure and tender moralist, but pusillanimous. He was so afraid of hurting and of being hurt, so afraid of running risks or tempting fortune, that he wished to prove that human life was a brief business, not subject to any great transformations, nor capable of any great achievements. He taught accordingly that the atoms had produced already all the animals they could produce, for though infinite in number the atoms were of few kinds. Consequently the possible sorts of being were finite and soon exhausted; this world, though on the eve of destruction, was of recent date. The worlds around it, or to be produced in future, could not afford anything essentially different. All the suns were much alike, and there was nothing new under them. We need not, then, fear the world; it is an explored and domestic scene,—a home, a little garden, six feet of earth for a man to stretch in. If people rage and make a great noise, it is not because there is much to win, or much to fear, but because people are mad. Let me not be mad, thought Epicurus; let me be reasonable, cultivating sentiments appropriate to a mortal who inhabits a world morally comfortable and small, and physically poor in its infinite monotony. The well-known lines of Fitzgerald echo this sentiment perfectly:

> *A Book of Verses underneath the Bough,*
> *A Jug of Wine, a Loaf of Bread—and Thou*
> *Beside me singing in the Wilderness—*
> *Oh, Wilderness were Paradise enow!*

But what if the shadow of incalculable possibilities should fall across this sunny retreat? What if after death we should awake in a world to which the atomic philosophy might not in the least apply? Observe that this suggestion is not in the least opposed to any of the arguments by which science might prove the atomic theory to be correct. All that Epicurus taught about the universe now before us might be perfectly true of it; but what if to-morrow a new universe should have taken its place? The suggestion is doubtless gratuitous, and no busy man will be much troubled by it; yet when the heart is empty it fills itself with such attenuated dreams. The muffled pleasures of the wise man, as Epicurus conceived him, were really a provocation to supernaturalism. They left a great void; and before long supernaturalism—we shall see it in Dante—actually rushed in to quicken the pulses of life with fresh hopes and illusions, or at least (what may seem better than nothing) with terrors and fanatical zeal. With such tendencies already afoot as the myths and dogmas of Plato had betrayed, it was imperative for Epicurus to banish anxiously all thought of what might follow death. To this end are all his arguments about the material nature of the soul and her incapacity to survive the body.

To say that the soul is material has a strange and barbarous sound to modern ears. We live after Descartes, who taught the world that the essence of the soul was consciousness; and to call consciousness material would be to talk of the blackness of white. But ancient usage gave the word soul a rather different meaning. The essence of the soul was not so much to be conscious as to govern the formation of the body, to warm, move, and guide it. And if we think of the soul exclusively in this light, it will not seem a paradox, it may even seem a truism, to say that the soul must be material. For how are we to conceive that preëxisting consciousness should govern the formation of the body, move, warm, or guide it? A spirit capable of such a miracle would in any case not be human, but altogether divine. The soul that Lucretius calls material should not, then, be identified with consciousness, but with the ground of consciousness, which is at the same time the cause of life in the body. This he conceives to be a swarm of very small and volatile atoms, a sort of ether, resident in all living seeds, breathed in abundantly during life and breathed out at death.

Even if this theory were accepted, however, it would not prove the point which Lucretius has chiefly at heart, namely, that an after-life is impossible. The atoms of the soul are indestructible, like all atoms; and if consciousness were attached to the fortunes of a small group of them, or of one only (as Leibniz afterwards taught), consciousness would continue to exist after these atoms had escaped from the body and were shooting through new fields of space. Indeed, they might be the more aroused by that adventure, as a bee might find the sky or the garden more exciting than the hive. All that Lucretius urges about the divisibility of the soul, its diffused bodily seat, and the perils it would meet outside fails to remove the ominous possibility that troubles him.

To convince us that we perish at death he has to rely on vulgar experience and inherent probability: what changes is not indestructible; what begins, ends; mental growth, health, sanity, accompany the fortunes of the body as a whole (not demonstrably those of the soul-atoms); the passions are relevant to bodily life and to an earthly situation; we should not be ourselves under a different mask or in a new setting; we remember no previous existence if we had one, and so, in a future existence, we should not remember this. These reflections are impressive, and they are enforced by Lucretius with his usual vividness and smack of reality. Nothing is proved scientifically by such a deliverance, yet it is good philosophy and good poetry; it brings much experience together and passes a lofty judgment upon it. The artist has his eye on the model; he is painting death to the life.

If these considerations succeed in banishing the dread of an after-life, there remains the distress which many feel at the idea of extinction; and if we have ceased to fear death, like Hamlet, for the dreams that may come after it, we may still fear death instinctively, like a stuck pig. Against this instinctive horror of dying Lucretius has many brave arguments. Fools, he says to us, why do you fear what never can touch you? While you still live, death is absent; and when you are dead, you are so dead that you cannot know you are dead, nor regret it. You will be as much at ease as before you were born. Or is what troubles you the childish fear of being cold in the earth, or feeling its weight stifling you? But you will not be there; the atoms of your soul—themselves unconscious—will be dancing in some sunbeam far away, and you yourself will be nowhere; you will absolutely not exist. Death is by definition a state that excludes experience. If you fear it, you fear a word.

To all this, perhaps, Memmius, or some other recalcitrant reader, might retort that what he shrank from was not the metaphysical state of being dead, but the very real agony of dying. Dying is something ghastly, as being born is something ridiculous; and, even if no pain were involved in quitting or entering this world, we might still say what Dante's Francesca says of it: *Il modo ancor m' offende,*—"I shudder at the way of it." Lucretius, for his part, makes no attempt to show that everything is as it should be; and if our way of coming into this life is ignoble, and our way of leaving it pitiful, that is no fault of his nor of his philosophy. If the fear of death were merely the fear of dying, it would be better dealt with by medicine than by argument. There is, or there might be, an art of dying well, of dying painlessly, willingly, and in season,—as in those noble partings which Attic gravestones depict,

—especially if we were allowed, as Lucretius would allow us, to choose our own time.

But the radical fear of death, I venture to think, is something quite different. It is the love of life. Epicurus, who feared life, seems to have missed here the primordial and colossal force he was fighting against. Had he perceived that force, he would have been obliged to meet it in a more radical way, by an enveloping movement, as it were, and an attack from the rear. The love of life is not something rational, or founded on experience of life. It is something antecedent and spontaneous. It is that Venus Genetrix which covers the earth with its flora and fauna. It teaches every animal to seek its food and its mate, and to protect its offspring; as also to resist or fly from all injury to the body, and most of all from threatened death. It is the original impulse by which good is discriminated from evil, and hope from fear.

Nothing could be more futile, therefore, than to marshal arguments against that fear of death which is merely another name for the energy of life, or the tendency to self-preservation. Arguments involve premises, and these premises, in the given case, express some particular form of the love of life; whence it is impossible to conclude that death is in no degree evil and not at all to be feared. For what is most dreaded is not the agony of dying, nor yet the strange impossibility that when we do not exist we should suffer for not existing. What is dreaded is the defeat of a present will directed upon life and its various undertakings. Such a present will cannot be argued away, but it may be weakened by contradictions arising within it, by the irony of experience, or by ascetic discipline. To introduce ascetic discipline, to bring out the irony of experience, to expose the self-contradictions of the will, would be the true means of mitigating the love of life; and if the love of life were extinguished, the fear of death, like smoke rising from that fire, would have vanished also.

Indeed, the force of the great passage against the fear of death, at the end of the third book of Lucretius, comes chiefly from the picture it draws of the madness of life. His philosophy deprecates covetousness, ambition, love, and religion; it takes a long step towards the surrender of life, by surrendering all in life that is ardent, on the ground that it is painful in the end and ignominious. To escape from it all is a great deliverance. And since genius must be ardent about something, Lucretius pours out his enthusiasm on Epicurus, who brought this deliverance and was the saviour of mankind. Yet this was only a beginning of salvation, and the same principles carried further would have delivered us from the Epicurean life and what it retained that was Greek and naturalistic: science, friendship, and the healthy pleasures of the body. Had it renounced these things also, Epicureanism would have become altogether ascetic, a thorough system of mortification, or the pursuit of death. To those who sincerely pursue death, death is no evil, but the highest good. No need in that case of elaborate arguments to prove that death should not be feared, because it is nothing; for in spite of being nothing—or rather because it is nothing— death can be loved by a fatigued and disillusioned spirit, just as in spite of being nothing—or rather because it is nothing—it must be hated and feared by every vigorous animal.

One more point, and I have done with this subject. Ancient culture was rhetorical. It abounded in ideas that are verbally plausible, and pass muster in a public speech, but that, if we stop to criticize them, prove at once to be inexcusably false. One of these rhetorical fallacies is the maxim that men cannot live for what they cannot witness. What does it matter to you, we may say in debate, what happened before you were born, or what may go on after you are buried? And the orator who puts such a challenge may carry the audience with him, and raise a laugh at the expense of human sincerity. Yet the very men who applaud are proud of their ancestors, care for the future of their children, and are very much interested in securing legally the execution of their last will and testament. What may go on after their death concerns them deeply, not because they expect to watch the event from hell or heaven, but because they are interested ideally in what that event shall be, although they are never to witness it. Lucretius himself, in his sympathy with nature, in his zeal for human enlightenment, in his tears for Iphigenia, long since dead, is not moved by the hope of observing, or the memory of having observed, what excites his emotion. He forgets himself. He sees the whole universe spread out in its true movement and proportions; he sees mankind freed from the incubus of superstition, and from the havoc of passion. The vision kindles his enthusiasm, exalts his imagination, and swells his verse into unmistakable earnestness.

If we follow Lucretius, therefore, in narrowing the sum of our personal fortunes to one brief and partial glimpse of earth, we must not suppose that we need narrow at all the sphere of our moral interests. On the contrary, just in proportion as we despise superstitious terrors and sentimental hopes, and as our imagination becomes self-forgetful, we shall strengthen the direct and primitive concern which we feel in the world and in what may go on there, before us, after us, or beyond our ken. If, like Lucretius and every philosophical poet, we range over all time and all existence, we shall forget our own persons, as he did, and even wish them to be forgotten, if only the things we care for may subsist or arise. He who truly loves God, says Spinoza, cannot wish that God should love him in return. One who lives the life of the universe cannot be much concerned for his own. After all, the life of the universe is but the locus and extension of ours. The atoms that have once served to produce life remain fit to reproduce it; and although the body they might animate later would be a new one, and would have a somewhat different career, it would not, according to Lucretius, be of a totally new species; perhaps not more unlike ourselves than we are unlike one another, or than each of us is unlike himself at the various stages of his life.

The soul of nature, in the elements of it, is then, according to Lucretius, actually immortal; only the human individuality, the chance composition of those elements, is transitory; so that, if a man could care for what happens to other men, for what befell him when young or what may overtake him when old, he might perfectly well care, on the same imaginative principle, for what may go on in the world for ever. The finitude and injustice of his personal life would be broken down; the illusion of selfishness would be dissipated; and he might say to himself, I have imagination, and nothing that is real is alien to me.

The word nature has many senses; but if we preserve the one which etymology justifies, and which is the most philosophical as well, nature should mean the principle of birth or genesis, the universal mother, the great cause, or system of causes, that brings phenomena to light. If we take the word nature in this sense, it may be said that Lucretius, more than any other man, is the poet of nature. Of course, being an ancient, he is not particularly a poet of landscape. He runs deeper than that; he is a poet of the source of landscape, a poet of matter. A poet of landscape might try to suggest, by well-chosen words, the sensations of light, movement, and form which nature arouses in us; but in this attempt he would encounter the insuperable difficulty which Lessing long ago pointed out, and warned poets of: I mean the unfitness of language to render what is spatial and material; its fitness to render only what, like language itself, is bodiless and flowing,—action, feeling, and thought.

It is noticeable, accordingly, that poets who are fascinated by pure sense and seek to write poems about it are called not impressionists, but symbolists; for in trying to render some absolute sensation they render rather the field of association in which that sensation lies, or the emotions and half-thoughts that shoot and play about it in their fancy. They become—against their will, perhaps—psychological poets, ringers of mental chimes, and listeners for the

chance overtones of consciousness. Hence we call
them symbolists, mixing perhaps some shade of dis-
paragement in the term, as if they were symbolists
of an empty, super-subtle, or fatuous sort. For they
play with things luxuriously, making them symbols
for their thoughts, instead of mending their thoughts
intelligently, to render them symbols for things.

A poet might be a symbolist in another sense,—
if he broke up nature, the object suggested by landscape to the mind, and reverted to the elements of
landscape, not in order to associate these sensations
lazily together, but in order to build out of them in
fancy a different nature, a better world, than that
which they reveal to reason. The elements of landscape, chosen, emphasized, and recombined for this
purpose, would then be symbols for the ideal world
they were made to suggest, and for the ideal life
that might be led in that paradise. Shelley is a symbolic landscape poet in this sense. To Shelley, as
Francis Thompson has said, nature was a toy-shop;
his fancy took the materials of the landscape and
wove them into a gossamer world, a bright ethereal
habitation for new-born irresponsible spirits. Shelley
was the musician of landscape; he traced out its unrealized suggestions; transformed the things he saw
into the things he would fain have seen. In this
idealization it was spirit that guided him, the bent
of his wild and exquisite imagination, and he fan-

cied sometimes that the grosser landscapes of earth
were likewise the work of some half-spiritual stress,
of some restlessly dreaming power. In this sense,
earthly landscape seemed to him the symbol of the
earth spirit, as the starlit crystal landscapes of his
verse, with their pensive flowers, were symbols in
which his own fevered spirit was expressed, images
in which his passion rested.

Another sort of landscape poetry is to be found
in Wordsworth, for whom the title of poet of nature
might perhaps be claimed. To him the landscape is
an influence. What he renders, beyond such pictorial
touches as language is capable of, is the moral inspiration which the scene brings to him. This moral
inspiration is not drawn at all from the real processes
of nature which every landscape manifests in some
aspect and for one moment. Such would have been
the method of Lucretius; he would have passed imaginatively from the landscape to the sources of the
landscape; he would have disclosed the poetry of
matter, not of spirit. Wordsworth, on the contrary,
dwells on adventitious human matters. He is no poet
of genesis, evolution, and natural force in its myriad
manifestations. Only a part of the cosmic process en-
gages his interest, or touches his soul—the strength-
ening or chastening of human purposes by the influences of landscape. These influences are very real;
for as food or wine keeps the animal heart beating,

or quickens it, so large spaces of calm sky, or mountains, or dells, or solitary stretches of water, expand the breast, disperse the obsessions that cramp a man's daily existence, and even if he be less contemplative and less virtuous than Wordsworth, make him, for the moment, a friend to all things, and a friend to himself.

Yet these influences are vague and for the most part fleeting. Wordsworth would hardly have felt them so distinctly and so constantly had he not found a further link to bind landscape to moral sentiment. Such a link exists. The landscape is the scene of human life. Every spot, every season, is associated with the sort of existence which falls to men in that environment. Landscape for Wordsworth's age and in his country was seldom without figures. At least, some visible trace of man guided the poet and set the key for his moral meditation. Country life was no less dear to Wordsworth than landscape was; it fitted into every picture; and while the march of things, as Lucretius conceived it, was not present to Wordsworth's imagination, the revolutions of society—the French Revolution, for instance—were constantly in his thoughts. In so far as he was a poet of human life, Wordsworth was truly a poet of nature. In so far, however, as he was a poet of landscape, he was still fundamentally a poet of human life, or merely of his personal experience. When he talked of nature he was generally moralizing, and altogether subject to the pathetic fallacy; but when he talked of man, or of himself, he was unfolding a part of nature, the upright human heart, and studying it in its truth.

Lucretius, a poet of universal nature, studied everything in its truth. Even moral life, though he felt it much more narrowly and coldly than Wordsworth did, was better understood and better sung by him for being seen in its natural setting. It is a fault of idealists to misrepresent idealism, because they do not view it as a part of the world. Idealism *is* a part of the world, a small and dependent part of it. It is a small and dependent part even in the life of men. This fact is nothing against idealism taken as a moral energy, as a faculty of idealization and a habit of living in the familiar presence of an image of what would, in everything, be best. But it is the ruin of idealism taken as a view of the central and universal power in the world. For this reason Lucretius, who sees human life and human idealism in their natural setting, has a saner and maturer view of both than has Wordsworth, for all his greater refinement. Nature, for the Latin poet, is really nature. He loves and fears her, as she deserves to be loved and feared by her creatures. Whether it be a wind blowing, a torrent rushing, a lamb bleating, the magic of love, genius achieving its purpose, or a war, or a pestilence,

Lucretius sees everything in its causes, and in its total career. One breath of lavish creation, one iron law of change, runs through the whole, making all things kin in their inmost elements and in their last end. Here is the touch of nature indeed, her largeness and eternity. Here is the true echo of the life of matter.

Any comprehensive picture of nature and destiny, if the picture be credited, must arouse emotion, and in a reflective and vivid mind must inspire poetry — for what is poetry but emotion, fixing and colouring the objects from which it springs? The sublime poem of Lucretius, expounding the least poetical of philosophies, proves this point beyond a doubt. Yet Lucretius was far from exhausting the inspiration which a poet might draw from materialism. In the philosophy of Epicurus, even, which had but a sickly hold on materialism, there were two strains which Lucretius did not take up, and which are naturally rich in poetry, the strain of piety and the strain of friendship. It is usual and, in one sense, legitimate to speak of the Epicureans as atheists, since they denied providence and any government of God in the world. Yet they admitted the existence of gods, living in the quiet spaces between those celestial whirlpools which form the various worlds. To these gods they attributed the human form, and the serene life to which Epicurus aspired. Epicurus himself was so sincere in this belief, and so much affected by it, that he used to frequent the temples, keep the feasts of the gods, and often spend hours before their images in contemplation and prayer.

In this, as in much else, Epicurus was carrying out to its logical conclusion the rational and reforming essence of Hellenism. In Greek religion, as in all other religions, there was a background of vulgar superstition. Survivals and revivals of totem-worship, taboo, magic, ritual barter, and objectified rhetoric are to be found in it to the very end; yet if we consider in Greek religion its characteristic tendency, and what rendered it distinctively Greek, we see that it was its unprecedented ideality, disinterestedness, and aestheticism. To the Greek, in so far as he was a Greek, religion was an aspiration to grow like the gods by invoking their companionship, rehearsing their story, feeling vicariously the glow of their splendid prerogatives, and placing them, in the form of beautiful and very human statues, constantly before his eyes. This sympathetic interest in the immortals took the place, in the typical Greek mind, of any vivid hope of human immortality; perhaps it made such a hope seem superfluous and inappropriate. Mortality belonged to man, as immortality to the gods; and the one was the complement of the other. Imagine a poet who, to the freedom and simplicity of Homer, should have added the more

reverent idealism of a later age; and what an inexhaustible fund of poetry might he not have
found in this conception of the immortals leading
a human life, without its sordid contrarieties and
limitations, eternally young, and frank, and different!

Hints of such poetry are to be found in Plato,
myths that present the ideal suggestions of human
life in pictures. These he sometimes leaves general
and pale, calling them ideas; but at other times he
embodies them in deities, or in detailed imaginary
constructions, like that of his *Republic.* This Platonic habit of mind might have been carried further
by some franker and less reactionary poet than Plato
was, or tended to become, as the years turned his
wine into vinegar. But the whole world was then
getting sour. Imagination flagged, or was diverted
from the Greek into the Hebrew channel. Nevertheless, the hymns of modern poets to the ancient
gods, and the irrepressible echoes of classic mythology in our literature, show how easy it would have
been for the later ancients themselves, had they
chosen, to make immortal poetry out of their dying
superstitions. The denials of Epicurus do not exclude this ideal use of religion; on the contrary, by
excluding all the other uses of it — the commercial,
the mock-scientific, and the selfish — they leave the
moral interpretative aspect of religion standing alone,

ready to the poet's hand, if any poet could be found pure and fertile enough to catch and to render it. Rationalized paganism might have had its Dante, a Dante who should have been the pupil not of Virgil and Aquinas, but of Homer and Plato. Lucretius was too literal, positivistic, and insistent for such a delicate task. He was a Roman. Moral mythology and ideal piety, though his philosophy had room for them, formed no part of his poetry.

What the other neglected theme, friendship, might have supplied, we may see in the tone of another Epicurean, the poet Horace. Friendship was highly honoured in all ancient states; and the Epicurean philosophy, in banishing so many traditional forms of sentiment, could only intensify the emphasis on friendship. It taught men that they were an accident in the universe, comrades afloat on the same raft together with no fate not common to them all, and no possible helpers but one another. Lucretius does speak, in a passage to which I have already referred,[1] about the hope of sweet friendship that supports him in his labours; and elsewhere[2] he repeats the Epicurean idyl about picnicking together

[1] Cf. pages 41, 42.
[2] Lucretius, II. 29-33:

> Inter se prostrati in gramine molli
> Propter aquae rivum, sub ramis arboris altae,
> Non magnis opibus iucunde corpora curant:
> Praesertim cum tempestas arridet, et anni
> Temra coponspergunt viridantis floribus herbas.

on the green grass by a flowing brook; but the little word "together" is all he vouchsafes us to mark what must be the chief ingredient in such rural happiness.

Horace, usually so much slighter than Lucretius, is less cursory here. Not only does he strike much oftener the note of friendship, but his whole mind and temper breathe of friendliness and expected agreement. There is, in the very charm and artifice of his lines, a sort of confidential joy in tasting with the kindred few the sweet or pungent savour of human things. To be brief and gently ironical is to assume mutual intelligence; and to assume mutual intelligence is to believe in friendship. In Lucretius, on the other hand, zeal is mightier than sympathy, and scorn mightier than humour. Perhaps it would be asking too much of his uncompromising fervour that he should have unbent now and then and shown us in some detail what those pleasures of life may be which are without care and fear. Yet, if it was impossible for him not to be always serious and austere, he might at least have noted the melancholy of friendship—for friendship, where nature has made minds isolated and bodies mortal, is rich also in melancholy. This again we may find in Horace, where once or twice he lets the "something bitter" bubble up from the heart even of this flower, when he feels a vague need that survives satiety, and

yearns perversely for the impossible.[1] Poor Epicureans, when they could not learn, like their master,
to be saints!

So far the decadent materialism of Epicurus might
have carried a poet; but a materialist in our days
might find many other poetic themes to weave into
his system. To the picture which Lucretius sketches
of primitive civilization, we might add the whole
history of mankind. To a consistent and vigorous
materialism all personal and national dramas, with
the beauties of all the arts, are no less natural and
interesting than are flowers or animal bodies. The
moral pageantry of this world, surveyed scientifically,
is calculated wonderfully to strengthen and refine
the philosophy of abstention suggested to Epicurus
by the flux of material things and by the illusions
of vulgar passion. Lucretius studies superstition, but
only as an enemy; and the naturalistic poet should
be the enemy of nothing. His animus blinds him to
half the object, to its more beautiful half, and makes
us distrust his version of the meaner half he is aware
of. Seen in its totality, and surrounded by all the
other products of human imagination, superstition
is not only moving in itself, a capital subject for
tragedy and for comedy, but it reinforces the ma-

---

1 Horace, *Odes*, IV. 1:

> Iam nec spes animi credula mutui . . .
> Sed cur, heu! Ligurine, cur
> Manat rara meas lacrima per genas?

terialistic way of thinking, and shows that it may be extended to the most complex and emotional spheres of existence. At the same time, a naturalism extended impartially over moral facts brings home a lesson of tolerance, scepticism, and independence which, without contradicting Epicurean principles, would very much enlarge and transform Epicurean sentiment. History would have opened to the Epicurean poet a new dimension of nature and a more varied spectacle of folly. His imagination would have been enriched and his maxims fortified.

The emotions which Lucretius associated with his atoms and void, with his religious denials and his abstentions from action, are emotions necessarily involved in life. They will exist in any case, though not necessarily associated with the doctrines by which this poet sought to clarify them. They will remain standing, whatever mechanism we put in the place of that which he believed in,— that is, if we are serious, and not trying to escape from the facts rather than to explain them. If the ideas embodied in a philosophy represent a comprehensive survey of the facts, and a mature sentiment in the presence of them, any new ideas adopted instead will have to acquire the same values, and nothing will be changed morally except the language or euphony of the mind.

Of course one theory of the world must be true

and the rest false, at least if the categories of any theory are applicable to reality; but the true theory like the false resides in imagination, and the truth of it which the poet grasps is its truth to life. If there are no atoms, at least there must be habits of nature, or laws of evolution, or dialectics of progress, or decrees of providence, or intrusions of chance; and before these equally external and groundless powers we must bow, as Lucretius bowed to his atoms. It will always be important and inevitable to recognize *something* external, something that generates or surrounds us; and perhaps the only difference between materialism and other systems in this respect is that materialism has studied more scrupulously the detail and method of our dependence.

Similarly, even if Lucretius was wrong, and the soul is immortal, it is nevertheless steadily changing its interests and its possessions. Our lives are mortal if our soul is not; and the sentiment which reconciled Lucretius to death is as much needed if we are to face many deaths, as if we are to face only one. The gradual losing of what we have been and are, Emerson says:

> *This losing is true dying;*
> *This is lordly man's down-lying,*
> *This his slow but sure reclining,*
> *Star by star his world resigning.*

The maxim of Lucretius, that nothing arises save

by the death of something else, meets us still in our crawling immortality. And his art of accepting and enjoying what the conditions of our being afford also has a perennial application. Dante, the poet of faith, will tell us that we must find our peace in the will that gives us our limited portion. Goethe, the poet of romantic experience, will tell us that we must renounce, renounce perpetually. Thus wisdom clothes the same moral truths in many cosmic parables. The doctrines of philosophers disagree where they are literal and arbitrary,—mere guesses about the unknown; but they agree or complete one another where they are expressive or symbolic, thoughts wrung by experience from the hearts of poets. Then all philosophies alike are ways of meeting and recording the same flux of images, the same vicissitudes of good and evil, which will visit all generations, while man is man.

DANTE

DANTE

IN the *Phaedo* of Plato there is an incidental passage of supreme interest to the historian. It foreshadows, and accurately defines, the whole transition from antiquity to the middle age, from naturalism to supernaturalism, from Lucretius to Dante. Socrates, in his prison, is addressing his disciples for the last time. The general subject is immortality; but in a pause in the argument Socrates says: "In my youth . . . I heard some one reading, as he said, from a book of Anaxagoras, that Reason was the disposer and cause of all, and I was delighted at this notion, which appeared quite admirable, and I said to myself: 'If Reason is the disposer, Reason will dispose all for the best, and put each particular in the best place;' and I argued that if any desired to find out the cause of the generation or destruction or existence of anything, he must find out what . . . was best for that thing. . . . And I rejoiced to think that I had found in Anaxagoras a teacher of the causes of existence such as I desired, and I imagined that he would tell me first whether the earth is flat or round; and whichever was true, he would proceed . . . to show the nature of the best, and show that this was best; and if he said that the earth was in the centre [of the universe], he would further ex-

plain that this position was the best, and I should be
satisfied with the explanation given, and not want
any other sort of cause. . . . For I could not imagine that when he spoke of Reason as the disposer
of things, he would give any other account of their
being, except that this was best. . . . These hopes
I would not have sold for a large sum of money, and
I seized the books and read them as fast as I could,
in my eagerness to know the better and the worse.

"What expectations I had formed and how griev-
ously was I disappointed! As I proceeded, I found
my philosopher altogether forsaking Reason or any
other principle of order, but having recourse to air,
and ether, and water, and other eccentricities. . . .
Thus one man makes a vortex all round, and steadies
the earth by the heaven; another gives the air as a
support to the earth, which is a sort of broad trough.
Any power which in arranging them as they are
arranges them for the best never enters into their
minds ; and instead of finding any superior strength
in it, they rather expect to discover another Atlas of
the world who is stronger and more everlasting and
more containing than the good; of the obligatory and
containing power of the good they think nothing;
and yet this is the principle which I would fain learn
if anyone would teach me."[1]

---

[1] Plato, *Phaedo*, 97 B–99 c, Jowett's translation. I have changed the rendering of νοῦς from "mind" to "reason."

Here we have the programme of a new philosophy. Things are to be understood by their uses or purposes, not by their elements or antecedents; as the fact that Socrates sits in his prison, when he might have escaped to Euboea, is to be understood by his allegiance to his notion of what is best, of his duty to himself and to his country, and not by the composition of his bones and muscles. Such reasons as we give for our actions, such grounds as might move the public assembly to decree this or that, are to be given in explanation of the order of nature. The world is a work of reason. It must be interpreted, as we interpret the actions of a man, by its motives. And these motives we must guess, not by a fanciful dramatic mythology, such as the poets of old had invented, but by a conscientious study of the better and the worse in the conduct of our own lives. For instance, the highest occupation, according to Plato, is the study of philosophy; but this would not be possible for man if he had to be continually feeding, like a grazing animal, with its nose to the ground. Now, to obviate the necessity of eating all the time, long intestines are useful; therefore the cause of long intestines is the study of philosophy. Again, the eyes, nose, and mouth are in the front of the head, because (says Plato) the front is the nobler side,—as if the back would not have been the nobler side (and the front side) had the eyes, nose, and mouth been there! This method is what Molière ridicules in *Le Malade Imaginaire*, when the chorus sings that opium puts people to sleep because it has a dormitive virtue, the nature of which is to make the senses slumber.

All this is ridiculous physics enough; but Plato knew—though he forgot sometimes—that his physics were playful. What it is important for us now to remember is rather that, under this childish or metaphorical physics, there is a serious morality. After all, the *use* of opium is that it is a narcotic; no matter why, physically, it is one. The *use* of the body *is* the mind, whatever the origin of the body may be. And it seems to dignify and vindicate these uses to say that they are the "causes" of the organs that make them possible. What is true of particular organs or substances is true of the whole frame of nature. Its *use* is to serve the good—to make life, happiness, and virtue possible. Therefore, speaking in parables, Plato says with his whole school: Discover the right principle of action, and you will have discovered the ruling force in the universe. Evoke in your rapt aspiration the essence of a supreme good, and you will have understood why the spheres revolve, why the earth is fertile, and why mankind suffers and exists. Observation must yield to dialectic; political art must yield to aspiration.

It took many hundred years for the revolution to

work itself out; Plato had a prophetic genius, and looked away from what he was (for he was a Greek) to what mankind was to become in the next cycle of civilization. In Dante the revolution is complete, not merely intellectually (for it had been completed intellectually long before, in the Neoplatonists and the Fathers of the Church), but complete morally and poetically, in that all the habits of the mind and all the sanctions of public life had been assimilated to it. There had been time to reinterpret everything, obliterating the natural lines of cleavage in the world, and substituting moral lines of cleavage for them. Nature was a compound of ideal purposes and inert matter. Life was a conflict between sin and grace. The environment was a battle-ground between a host of angels and a legion of demons. The better and the worse had actually become, as Socrates desired, the sole principles of understanding.

Having become Socratic, the thinking part of mankind devoted all its energies henceforward to defining good and evil in all their grades, and in their ultimate essence; a task which Dante brings to a perfect conclusion. So earnestly and exclusively did they speculate about moral distinctions that they saw them in almost visible shapes, as Plato had seen his ideas. They materialized the terms of their moral philosophy into existing objects and powers. The highest good—in Plato still chiefly a political ideal, the aim of policy and art—became God, the creator of the world. The various stages or elements of perfection became persons in the Godhead, or angelic intelligences, or aerial demons, or lower types of the animal soul. Evil was identified with matter. The various stages of imperfection were ascribed to the grossness of various bodies, which weighted and smothered the spark of divinity that animated them. This spark, however, might be released; then it would fly up again to its parent fire and a soul would be saved.

This philosophy was not a serious description of nature or evolution; but it was a serious judgement upon them. The good, the better, the best, had been discerned; and a mythical bevy of powers, symbolizing these degrees of excellence, had been first talked of and then believed in. Myth, when another man has invented it, can pass for history; and when this man is a Plato, and has lived long ago, it can pass for revelation. In this way moral values came to be regarded as forces working in nature. But if they worked in nature, which was a compound of evil matter and perfect form, they must exist outside: for the ideal of excellence beckons from afar; it is what we pine for and are not. The forces that worked in nature were accordingly supernatural virtues, dominations, and powers; each natural thing had its supernatural incubus, a guardian angel, or a devil that possessed it. The supernatural—that is, something moral or ideal regarded as a power and an existence—was all about us. Everything in the world was an effect of something beyond the world; everything in life was a step to something beyond life.

Into this system Christianity fitted easily. It enriched it by adding miraculous history to symbolic cosmology. The Platonists had conceived a cosmos in which there were higher and lower beings, marshalled in concentric circles, around this vile but pivotal lump of earth. The Christians supplied a dramatic action for which that stage seemed admirably fitted, a story in which the whole human race, or the single soul, passed successively through these higher and lower stages. There had been a fall, and there might be a salvation. In a sense, even this conception of descent from the good, and ascent towards it again, was Platonic. According to the Platonists, the good eternally shed its vital influence, like light, and received (though unawares and without increase of excellence to itself) reflected rays that, in the form of love and thought, reverted to it from the ends of the universe. But according to the Platonist this radiation of life and focusing of aspiration were both perpetual. The double movement was eternal. The history of the world was monotonous; or rather the world had no significant history, but only a movement like that of a fountain playing for ever, or like the circulation of water that is always falling from the clouds in rain and always rising again in vapour. This fall, or emanation of the world from the deity, was the origin of evil for the Platonists; evil consisted merely in finitude, materiality, or otherness from God. If anything besides God was to exist, it had to be imperfect; instability and conflict were essential to finitude and to existence. Salvation, on the other hand, was the return current of aspiration on the part of the creature to revert to its source; an aspiration which was expressed in various types of being, fixed in the eternal,—types which led up, like the steps of a temple, to the ineffable good at the top.

In the Christian system this cosmic circulation became only a figure or symbol expressing the true creation, the true fall, and the true salvation; all three being really episodes in a historical drama, occurring only once. The material world was only a scene, a stage-setting, designed expressly to be appropriate for the play; and this play was the history of mankind, especially of Israel and of the Church. The persons and events of this history had a philosophic import; each played some part in a providential plan. Each illustrated creation, sin, and salvation in some degree, and on some particular level.

The Jews had never felt uncomfortable at being material; even in the other world they hoped to re-

main so, and their immortality was a resurrection of
the flesh. It did not seem plausible to them that this
excellent frame of things should be nothing but a
faint, troubled, and unintended echo of the good. On
the contrary, they thought this world so good, intrinsically, that they were sure God must have made
it expressly, and not by an unconscious effluence of
his virtue, as the Platonists had believed. Their wonder at the power and ingenuity of the deity reached
its maximum when they thought of him as the cun-
ning contriver of nature, and of themselves. Nevertheless the work seemed to show some imperfections;
indeed, its moral excellence was potential rather
than actual, a suggestion of what might be, rather
than an accomplished fact. And so, to explain the
unexpected flaws in a creation which they thought
essentially good, they put back at the beginning of
things an experience they had daily in the present,
namely, that trouble springs from bad conduct.

The Jews were intent watchers of fortune and of
its vicissitudes. The careers of men were their meditation by day and by night; and it takes little attention to perceive that frivolity, indifference, knavery,
and debauchery do not make for well-being in this
world. And like other hard-pressed peoples, the ancient Jews had a pathetic admiration for safety and
plenty. How little they must have known these
things, to think of them so rapturously and so poet-

ically! Not merely their personal prudence, but their corporate and religious zeal made them abhor that bad conduct which defeated prosperity. It was not mere folly, but wickedness and the abomination of desolation. With the lessons of conduct continually in mind, they framed the theory that all suffering, and even death, were the wages of sin. Finally they went so far as to attribute evil in all creation to the casual sin of a first man, and to the taint of it transmitted to his descendants; thus passing over the suffering and death of all creatures that are not human with an indifference that would have astonished the Hindoos.

The imperfection of things, in the Hebraic view, was due to accidents in their operation; not, as in the Platonic view, to their essential separation from their source and their end. It is in harmony with this that salvation too should come by virtue of some special act, like the incarnation or death of Christ. Just so, the Jews had conceived salvation as a revival of their national existence and greatness, to be brought about by the patience and fidelity of the elect, with tremendous miracles supervening to reward these virtues.

Thus their conception of the fall and of the redemption was historical. And this was a great advantage to a man of imagination inheriting their system; for the personages and the miracles that

figured in their sacred histories afforded a rich subject for fancy to work upon, and for the arts to depict. The patriarchs from Adam down, the kings
and prophets, the creation, Eden, the deluge, the
deliverance out of Egypt, the thunders and the law
of Sinai, the temple, the exile—all this and much
more that fills the Bible was a rich fund, a familiar
tradition living in the Church, on which Dante could
draw, as he drew at the same time from the parallel
classic tradition which he also inherited. To lend all
these Biblical persons and incidents a philosophical
dignity he had only to fit them, as the Fathers of the
Church had done, into the Neoplatonic cosmology,
or, as the doctors of his own time were doing, into
the Aristotelian ethics.

So interpreted, sacred history acquired for the philosopher a new importance besides that which it
had seemed to have to Israel in exile, or to the
Christian soul conscious of sin. Every episode became the symbol for some moral state or some moral
principle. Every preacher in Christendom, as he repeated his homily on the gospel of the day, was in-
vited to rear a structure of spiritual interpretations
upon the literal sense of the narrative, which nevertheless he was always to hold and preserve as a
foundation for the others.[1] In a world made by God

---

[1] "Est pro fundamento tenenda veritas historiae et desuper spirituales ex-
positiones fabricandae." Thomas Aquinas, *Summa Theologiae*, I. quaest. 102,
conclusio.

for the illustration of his glory, things and events, though real, must be also symbolical; for there is intention and propriety behind them. The creation, the deluge, the incarnation, crucifixion, and resurrection of Christ, the coming of the Holy Ghost with flames of fire and the gift of tongues, were all historical facts. The Church was heir to the chosen people; it was an historic and political institution, with a destiny in this world, in which all her children should share, and for which they should fight. At the same time all those facts were mysteries and sacraments for the private soul; they were channels for the same moral graces that were embodied in the order of the heavenly spheres, and in the types of moral life on earth. Thus the Hebrew tradition brought to Dante's mind the consciousness of a providential history, a great earthly task,—to be transmitted from generation to generation,—and a great hope. The Greek tradition brought him natural and moral philosophy. These contributions, joined together, had made Christian theology.

Although this theology was the guide to Dante's imagination, and his general theme, yet it was not his only interest; or rather he put into the framework of orthodox theology theories and visions of his own, fusing all into one moral unity and one poetical enthusiasm. The fusion was perfect between the personal and the traditional elements. He threw politics and love into the melting-pot, and they, too, lost their impurities and were refined into a philosophic religion. Theology became, to his mind, the guardian of patriotism, and, in a strangely literal sense, the angel of love.

The political theory of Dante is a sublime and largely original one. It suffers only from its extreme ideality, which makes it inapplicable, and has caused it to be studied less than it deserves.

A man's country, in the modern sense, is something that arose yesterday, that is constantly changing its limits and its ideals; it is something that cannot last for ever. It is the product of geographical and historical accidents. The diversities between our different nations are irrational; each of them has the same right, or want of right, to its peculiarities. A man who is just and reasonable must nowadays, so far as his imagination permits, share the patriotism of the rivals and enemies of his country,—a patriotism as inevitable and pathetic as his own. Nationality being an irrational accident, like sex or complexion, a man's allegiance to his country must be conditional, at least if he is a philosopher. His patriotism has to be subordinated to rational allegiance to such things as justice and humanity.

Very different was the situation in Dante's case. For him the love of country could be something absolute, and at the same time something reasonable, deliberate, and moral. What he found claiming his allegiance was a political body quite ideal, providential, and universal. This political body had two heads, like the heraldic eagle,—the pope and the emperor. Both were, by right, universal potentates; both should have their seat in Rome; and both should direct their government to the same end, although by different means and in different spheres. The pope should watch over the faith and discipline of the Church. He should bear witness, in all lands and ages, to the fact that life on earth was merely a preliminary to existence in the other world, and should be a preparation for that. The emperor, on the other hand, should guard peace and justice everywhere, leaving to free cities or princes the regulation of local affairs. These two powers had been established by God through special miracles and commissions. An evident providential design, culminating in them, ran through all history.

To betray or resist these divine rights, or to confound them, was accordingly a sin of the first magnitude. The evils from which society suffered were the consequence of such transgressions. The pope had acquired temporal power, which was alien to his purely spiritual office; besides, he had become a tool of the French king, who was (what no king should be) at war with the emperor, and rebellious against

the supreme imperial authority; indeed, the pope had
actually been seen to abandon Rome for Avignon,
—an act which was a sort of satanic sacrament, the
outward sign of an inward disgrace. The emperor,
in his turn, had forgotten that he was King of the
Romans and Caesar, and was fond of loitering in his
native Germany, among its forests and princelings,
as if the whole world were not by right his country,
and the object of his solicitude.

And here the larger, theoretical patriotism of
Dante, as a Catholic and a Roman, passed into his
narrower and actual patriotism as a Florentine.
Had Florence been true to its duties and worthy
of its privileges, under the double authority of the
Church and the Empire? Florence was a Roman
colony. Had it maintained the purity of its Roman
stock, and a Roman simplicity and austerity in its
laws? Alas, Etruscan immigrants had contaminated
its blood, and this taint was responsible, Dante
thought, for the prevalent corruption of manners.
All that has made Florence great in the history of
the world was then only just beginning,—its industry, refinements, arts, and literature. But to Dante
that budding age seemed one of decadence and
moral ruin. He makes his ancestor, the crusader
Cacciaguida, praise the time when the narrow cir-
cuit of the walls held only one-fifth of its later in-
habitants. "Then the city abided in peace, sober

and chaste."[1] The women plied the distaff, or rocked
the cradle, and prattled to their children of the heroic
legends of Troy, Fiesole, and Rome. A woman could
turn from her glass with her face unpainted; she wore
no girdle far more deserving of admiration than her
own person. The birth of a daughter did not frighten
a good burgher; her dowry would not have to be excessive, nor her marriage premature. No houses were
empty, their masters being in exile; none were dis-
graced by unmentionable orgies.[2] This was not all;
for if luxury was a great curse to Florence, faction
was a greater. Florence, an imperial city, far from
assisting in the restitution of the emperors to their
universal rights, had fought against them traitorously,

[1] *Paradiso*, xv. 97, 99 :

> Fiorenza dentro dalla cerchia antica . . .
> Si stava in pace, sobria e pudica.

[2] Ibid., 100–26 :

> Non avea catenella, non corona,
>   Non donne contigiate, non cintura
>   Che fosse a veder più che la persona.
> Non faceva nascendo ancor paura
>   La figlia al padre, chè il tempo e la dote
>   Non fuggían quinci e quindi la misura.
> Non avea case di famiglia vote;
>   Non v' era giunto ancor Sardanapalo
>   A mostrar ciò che in camera si puote. . . .
> O fortunate! Ciascuna era certa
>   Della sua sepoltura, ed ancor nulla
>   Era per Francia nel letto deserta.
> L' una vegghiava a studio della culla,
>   E consolando usava l' idioma
>   Che prima i padri e le madri trastulla;
> L' altra traendo alla rocca la chioma,
>   Favoleggiava con la sua famiglia
>   De' Troiani, di Fiesole, e di Roma.

in alliance with the French invader and the usurping pontiff. It had thus undermined the only possible foundation of its own peace and dignity.

These were the theoretical sorrows that loomed behind the personal sorrows of Dante in his poverty and exile. They helped him to pour forth the intense bitterness of his heart with the breath of prophetic invective. They made his hatred of the actual popes and of the actual Florence so much fervid zeal for what the popes and Florence ought to have been. His political passions and political hopes were fused with a sublime political ideal; that fusion sublimated them, and made it possible for the expression of them to rise into poetry.

Here is one iron string on which Dante played, and which gave a tragic strength to his music. He recorded the villainies of priests, princes, and peoples. He upbraided them for their infidelity to the tasks assigned to them by God,—tasks which Dante conceived with a Biblical definiteness and simplicity. He lamented the consequences of this iniquity, wasted provinces, corrupted cities, and the bodies of heroes rolling unburied down polluted streams. These vigorous details were exalted by the immense significance that Dante infused into them. His ever-present definite ideal quickened his eye for the ebb and flow of things, rendered the experience of them singly more poignant, and the vision of them together more sustained and cumulative. Dante read contemporary Italy as the Hebrew prophets read the signs of their times; and whatever allowance our critical judgement may make for generous illusions on the part of either, there can be no doubt that their wholeness of soul, and the prophetic absoluteness of their judgements, made their hold on particular facts very strong, and their sense for impending weal or woe quite overpowering.

Nor does it seem that at bottom Dante's political philosophy, any more than that of the Hebrew prophets, missed the great causes and the great aims of human progress. Behind mythical and narrow conceptions of history, he had a true sense for the moral principles that really condition our well-being. A better science need subtract nothing from the insight he had into the difference between political good and evil. What in his day seemed a dream—that mankind should be one great commonwealth—is now obvious to the idealist, the socialist, the merchant. Science and trade are giving, in a very different form, to be sure, a practical realization to that idea. And the other half of his theory, that of the Catholic Church, is maintained literally by that church itself to this day; and the outsider might see in that ideal of a universal spiritual society a symbol or premonition of the right of the mind to freedom from legal compulsions, or of the common allegiance of honest minds to science, and to their common spiritual heritage and destiny.

On the other hand, the sting of Dante's private wrongs, like the enthusiasm of his private loves, lent a wonderful warmth and clearness to the great objects of his imagination. We are too often kept from feeling great things greatly for want of power to assimilate them to the little things which we feel keenly and sincerely. Dante had, in this respect, the art of a Platonic lover: he could enlarge the object of his passion, and keep the warmth and ardour of it undiminished. He had been banished unjustly — *Florentinus exul immeritus*, he liked to call himself. That injustice rankled, but it did not fester, in his heart; for his indignation spread to all wrong, and thundered against Florence, Europe, and mankind, in that they were corrupt and perfidious. Dante had loved. The memory of that passion remained also, but it did not degenerate into sentimentality; for his adoration passed to a larger object and one less accidental. His love had been a spark of that "love which moves the sun and the other stars."[1] He had known, in that revelation, the secret of the universe. The spheres, the angels, the sciences, were henceforth full of sweetness, comfort, and light.

---

[1] *Paradiso*, xxxiii. 143–45:

> Volgeva il mio disiro e il *velle*,
> Sì come rota ch' egualmente è mossa,
> L' amor che move il sole e l' altre stelle.

Of this Platonic expansion of emotion, till it suffuses all that deserves to kindle it, we have a wonderful version in Dante's *Vita Nuova*. This book, on the surface, is an account of Dante's meeting, at the age of nine, with Beatrice, a child even a little younger; of another meeting with her at the age of eighteen; of an overwhelming mystic passion which the lover wished to keep secret, so much so that he feigned another attachment as a blind; of a consequent estrangement; and of the death of Beatrice, whereupon the poet resolved not to speak publicly of her again, until he could praise her in such wise as no woman had ever been praised before.

This story is interspersed with poems of the most exquisite delicacy, both in sentiment and in versification. They are dreamlike, allegorical, musical meditations, ambiguous in their veiled meanings, but absolutely clear and perfect in their artful structure, like a work of tracery and stained glass, geometrical, mystical, and tender. A singular limpidity of accent and image, a singular naïveté, is strangely combined in these pieces with scholastic distinctions and a delight in hiding and hinting, as in a charade.

The learned will dispute for ever on the exact basis and meaning of these confessions of Dante. The learned are perhaps not those best fitted to solve the problem. It is a matter for literary tact and sympathetic imagination. It must be left to the delicate intelligence of the reader, if he has it; and if he has not, Dante does not wish to open his heart to him. His enigmatical manner is his protection against the intrusion of uncongenial minds.

Without passing beyond the sphere of learned criticism, I think we may say this: the various interpretations, in this matter, are not mutually exclusive. Symbolism and literalness, in Dante's time, and in his practice, are simultaneous. For instance, in any history of mediaeval philosophy you may read that a great subject of dispute in those days was the question whether universal terms or natures, such as man, or humanity, existed before the particulars, in the particulars, or after the particulars, by abstraction of what was common to them all. Now, this matter was undoubtedly much disputed about; but there is one comprehensive and orthodox solution, which represents the true mind of the age, above the peculiar hobbies or heresies of individuals. This solution is that universal terms or natures exist before the particulars, *and* in the particulars, *and* after the particulars: for God, before he made the world, knew how he intended to make it, and had eternally in his mind the notions of a perfect man, horse, etc., after which the particulars were to be modelled, or to which, in case of accident, they were to be restored, either by the healing and recuperative force of nature, or by the ministrations of grace.

But universal terms or natures existed also *in* the particulars, since the particulars illustrated them, shared in them, and were what they were by virtue of that participation. Nevertheless, the universals existed also after the particulars: for the discursive mind of man, surveying the variety of natural things, could not help noticing and abstracting the common types that often recur in them; and this *ex post facto* idea, in the human mind, is a universal term also. To deny any of the three theories, and not to see their consistency, is to miss the mediaeval point of view, which, in every sense of the word, was Catholic.

Just such a solution seems to me natural in the case of Beatrice. We have it on independent documentary evidence that in Dante's time there actually lived in Florence a certain Bice Portinari; and there are many incidents in the *Vita Nuova* and in the *Commedia* which hardly admit of an allegorical interpretation; such as the death of Beatrice, and especially that of her father, on which occasion Dante writes a sympathetic poem.[1] I can see no reason why this lady, as easily as any other person, should not have called forth the dreamful passion of our poet.

---

[1] *Vita Nuova*, § 22: Secondo l' usanza della sopradetta cittade, donne con donne, e uomini con uomini si adunino a cotale tristizia; molte donne s' adunaro colà, ove questa Beatrice piangea pietosamente, &c.

Also, *Purgatorio*, xxxi. 50, 51:

> Le belle membra in ch' io
> Rinchiusa fui, e sono in terra sparte.

That he had loved some one is certain. Most people
have; and why should Dante, in particular, have
found the language of love a natural veil for his
philosophy, if the passion and the language of love
had not been his mother-tongue? The language of
love is no doubt usual in the allegories of mystics,
and was current in the conventional poetry of Dante's
time; but mystics themselves are commonly crossed
or potential lovers; and the troubadours harped on
the string of love simply because it was the most re-
sponsive string in their own natures, and that which
could most easily be made to vibrate in their hearers.
Dante was not less sensitive than the average man
of his generation; and if he followed the fashion of
minstrels and mystics, it was because he shared their
disposition. The beautiful, the unapproachable, the
divine, had passed before him in some visible form;
it matters nothing whether this vision came once
only, and in the shape of the actual Beatrice, or con-
tinuously, and in every shape through which a divine
influence may seem to come to a poet. No one would
deserve this name of poet—and who deserves it more
than Dante?—if real sights and sounds never impressed him; and he would hardly deserve it either,
if they impressed him only physically, and for what
they are in themselves. His sensibility creates his
ideal.

If to deny the existence of an historical Beatrice

seems violent and gratuitous, it would be a much
worse misunderstanding not to perceive that Beatrice is *also* a symbol. On one occasion, as we read
in the *Vita Nuova*,[1] Dante found himself, in a
church, in the presence of Beatrice. His eyes were
inevitably fixed upon her; but as he wished to con-
ceal his profound passion from the gossiping crowd,
he chose another lady, who happened to stand in the
direct line of vision between him and Beatrice, and
pretended to be gazing at her, in reality looking beyond her to Beatrice. This intervening lady, *la donna
gentile*, became the screen to his true love.[2] But
his attentions to her were so assiduous that they
were misinterpreted. Beatrice herself observed them,
and thinking he was going too far and not with an
honourable purpose, showed her displeasure by refus-
ing to greet him as he passed. This sounds real and
earthly enough : but what is our surprise when we
read expressly, in the *Convito,* that the *donna gentile,*
the screen to Dante's true love, is philosophy.[3] If the

---

[1] *Vita Nuova*, § v.

[2] *Schermo della veritade,* — natural philosophy.

[3] *Convito,* ii. cap. 16 : *Faccia che gli occhi d' esta Donna miri;* gli occhi di
questa Donna sono le sue *dimostrazioni,* le quali dritte negli occhi dello
intelletto innamorano l' anima, libera nelle condizioni. Oh dolcissimi ed
ineffabili sembianti, e rubatori subitani della mente umana, che nelle
dimostrazioni negli occhi della Filosofia apparite, quando essa alli suoi
drudi ragiona ! Veramente in voi è la salute, per la quale si fa beato chi
vi guarda, e salvo dalla morte della ignoranza e delli vizi. . . . E così, in
fine di questo secondo Trattato, dico e affermo che la Donna, di cui io in-
namorai appresso lo primo amore, fu la bellissima e onestissima figlia dello
Imperadore dell' universo, alla quale Pittagora pose nome *Filosofia.*

donna gentile is philosophy, the *donna gentilissima,* Beatrice, must be something of the same sort, only nobler. She must be theology, and theology Beatrice undoubtedly is. Her very name is played upon, if not selected, to mean that she is what renders blessed, what shows the path of salvation.

Now the scene in the church becomes an allegory throughout. The young Dante, we are given to understand, was at heart a religious and devout soul, looking for the highest wisdom. But intervening between his human reason and revealed truth (which he really was in love with, and wished to win and to understand) he found philosophy or, as we should say, science. To science he gave his preliminary attention; so much so that the mysteries of theology were momentarily obscured in his mind; and his faith, to his great sorrow, refused to salute him as he passed. He had fallen into materialistic errors; he had interpreted the spots on the moon as if they could be due to physical, not to Socratic, causes; and his religious philosophy had lost its warmth, even if his religious faith had not actually been endangered. It is certain, then, that Beatrice, besides being a woman, was also a symbol.

But this is not the end. If Beatrice is a symbol for theology, theology itself is not final. It, too, is an avenue, an interpretation. The eyes of Beatrice reflect a supernal light. It is the ineffable vision of

God, the beatific vision, that alone can make us happy
and be the reason and the end of our loves and our
pilgrimages.

A supreme ideal of peace and perfection which
moves the lover, and which moves the sky, is more
easily named than understood. In the last canto of
the *Paradiso*, where Dante is attempting to describe
the beatific vision, he says many times over that
our notion of this ideal must be vague and inade-
quate. The value of the notion to a poet or a philosopher does not lie in what it contains positively, but in
the attitude which it causes him to assume towards
real experience. Or perhaps it would be better to say
that to have an ideal does not mean so much to have
any image in the fancy, any Utopia more or less
articulate, but rather to take a consistent moral attitude towards all the things of this world, to judge
and coördinate our interests, to establish a hierarchy
of goods and evils, and to value events and persons,
not by a casual personal impression or instinct, but
according to their real nature and tendency. So understood, an ultimate ideal is no mere vision of the
philosophical dreamer, but a powerful and passionate
force in the poet and the orator. It is the voice of his
love or hate, of his hope or sorrow, idealizing, chal-
lenging, or condemning the world.

It is here that the feverish sensibility of the young
Dante stood him in good stead; it gave an unpre-

cedented vigour and clearness to his moral vision; it made him the classic poet of hell and of heaven. At the same time, it helped to make him an upright judge, a terrible accuser, of the earth. Everything and everybody in his day and generation became to him, on account of his intense loyalty to his inward vision, an instance of divine graciousness or of devilish perversity. Doubtless this keenness of soul was not wholly due to the gift of loving, or to the discipline of love; it was due in part also to pride, to resentment, to theoretical prejudices. But figures like that of Francesca di Rimini and Manfred, and the light and rapture vibrating through the whole *Paradiso*, could hardly have been evoked by a merely irritated genius. The background and the starting-point of everything in Dante is the *intelletto d' amore*, the genius of love.

Everybody has heard that God is love and that love makes the world go round; and those who have traced this latter notion back to its source in Aristotle may have some notion of what it means. It means, as we saw in the beginning, that we should not try to explain motion and life by their natural antecedents, for these run back *in infinitum*. We should explain motion and life rather by their purpose or end, by that unrealized ideal which moving and living things seem to aspire to, and may be said to love. What justifies itself is not any fact or law; for why should these not have been different? What justifies itself is what is good, what is as it ought to be. But things in motion, Aristotle conceived, declare, as it were, that they are not satisfied, and ought to be in some different condition. They look to a fulfilment which is as yet ideal. This fulfilment, if it included motion and life, could include them inwardly only; it would consist in a sustained activity, never lapsing nor suffering change. Such an activity is the unchanging goal towards which life advances and by which its different stages are measured. But since the purpose of things, and not their natural causes, is that which explains them, we may call this eventual activity their reason for being. It will be their unmoved mover.

But how, we may ask,—how can the unchanging, the ideal, the eventual, initiate anything or determine the disposition and tendency of what actually lives and moves? The answer, or rather the impossibility of giving an answer, may be expressed in a single word: magic. It is magic when a good or interesting result, because it would prove good or interesting, is credited with marshalling the conditions and evoking the beings that are to realize it. It is natural that I should be hungry, and natural that there should be things suitable for me to eat—for otherwise I should not be hungry long; but if my hunger, in case it is sharp enough, should be able of itself to produce the food it calls for, that would be magic. Nature would be evoked by the incantations of the will.

I do not forget that Aristotle, with Dante after him, asserts that the goal of life is a separate being already existing, namely, the mind of God, eternally realizing what the world aspires to. The influence of this mind, however, upon the world is no less magical than would be that of a non-existent ideal. For its operation is admittedly not transitive or physical. It itself does not change in working. No virtue leaves it; it does not, according to Aristotle and Plotinus, even know that it works. Indeed, it works only because other things are disposed to pursue it as their ideal; let things keep this disposition, and they will pursue and frame their ideal no less if it nowhere has an actual existence, than if by chance it exists elsewhere in its own person. It works only in its capacity of ideal; therefore, even if it exists, it works only by magic. The matter beneath feels the spell of its presence, and catches something of its image, as the waves of the sea might receive and reflect tremblingly the light shed by the moon. The world accordingly is moved and vivified in every fibre by magic, by the magic of the goal to which it aspires.

But this magic, on earth, bore the name of love. The life of the world was a love, produced by the magic attraction of a good it has never possessed and, so long as it remains a world, is incapable of possessing. Actual things were only suggestions of what the elements in that ulterior existence ought to be: they were mere symbols. The acorn was a mere prophecy—an existing symbol—for the ideal oak; because when the acorn falls into good ground it will be corrupted, but the idea of the oak will arise and be manifested in its place. The acorn was a sort of reliquary in which the miraculous power of the idea was somehow enshrined. In the vulgar attribution of causes we, like Anaxagoras, resemble a superstitious relic-worshipper who should forget that the intercession and merits of the saint really work the miracle, and should attribute it instead to the saint's bones and garments in their material capacity. Similarly, we should attribute the power which things exerted over us, not to the rarer or denser substance, but to the eternal ideas that they existed by expressing, and existed to express. Things merely localized—like the saint's relics—the influences which flowed to us from above. In the world of values they were mere symbols, accidental channels for divine energy; and since divine energy, by its magic assimilation of matter, had created these things, in order to express itself, they were symbols altogether not merely in their use, but in their origin and nature.

A mind persuaded that it lives among things that, like words, are essentially significant, and that what they signify is the magic attraction, called love, which draws all things after it, is a mind poetic in its intuition, even if its language be prose. The science and philosophy of Dante did not have to be put into verse in order to become poetry: they were poetry fundamentally and in their essence. When Plato and Aristotle, following the momentous precept of Socrates, decreed that observation of nature should stop and a moral interpretation of nature should begin, they launched into the world a new mythology, to take the place of the Homeric one which was losing its authority. The power the poets had lost of producing illusion was possessed by these philosophers in a high degree; and no one was ever more thoroughly under their spell than Dante. He became to Platonism and Christianity what Homer had been to Paganism; and if Platonism and Christianity, like Paganism, should ever cease to be defended scientifically, Dante will keep the poetry and wisdom of them alive; and it is safe to say that later generations will envy more than they will despise his philosophy. When the absurd controversies and factious passions that in some measure obscure the nature of this system have completely passed away, no one will think of reproaching Dante with his bad science, and bad history, and minute theology. These will not seem blemishes in his poetry, but integral parts of it.

A thousand years after Homer, Alexandrian critics

were expounding his charming myths as if they were
a revealed treatise of physics and morals. A thousand years after Dante we may hope that his conscientious vision of the universe, where all is love,
magic, and symbolism, may charm mankind exclusively as poetry. So conceived, the *Divine Comedy*
marks high noon in that long day-dream of which
Plato's dialogues mark the beginning: a pause of two
thousand years in the work of political reason, during which the moral imagination spun out of itself
an allegorical philosophy, as a boy, kept at home
during a rainy day with books too hard and literal
for his years, might spin his own romance out of
his father's histories, and might define, with infantile
precision, his ideal lady-love, battles, and kingdoms.
The middle age saw the good in a vision. It is for
the new age to translate those delightful symbols into the purposes of manhood.

In a letter which tradition assigns to Dante, addressed to his protector, Cangrande della Scala, lord
of Verona and Vicenza, are these words about the
Divine Comedy: "The subject of the whole work,
taken merely in its literal sense, is the state of souls
after death, considered simply as a fact. But if the
work is understood in its allegorical intention, the
subject of it is man, according as, by his deserts and
demerits in the use of his free will, he is justly open

to rewards and punishments." This by no means exhausts, however, the significations which we may look for in a work of Dante's. How many these may be is pointed out to us in the same letter, and illustrated by the beginning of the one hundred and fourteenth Psalm: "When Israel went out of Egypt, the house of Jacob from a people of strange language; Judah was his sanctuary, and Israel his dominion." Here, Dante tells us, "if we look to the *letter* only, what is conveyed to us is the deliverance of the children of Israel out of Egypt in the time of Moses; if we look to the *allegory* of it, what is signified is our redemption accomplished through Christ; if we consider the *moral sense*, what is signified is the conversion of the soul from her present grief and wretchedness to a state of grace; and if we consider the *anagogical sense* [that is, the revelation contained concerning our highest destiny], what is signified is the passing of the sanctified soul from the bondage of earthly corruption to the freedom of everlasting glory."

When people brooded so much over a simple text as to find all these meanings in it, we may expect that their own works, when meant to be profound, should have stage above stage of allegorical application. So in the first canto of the *Inferno* we find a lion that keeps Dante from approaching a delectable mountain; and this lion, besides what he is in the landscape of the poem, is a symbol for pride or power in general, for the king of France in particular, and for whatever political ambitions in Dante's personal life may have robbed him of happiness or distracted him from faith and from piety. Thus, throughout the *Divine Comedy*, meaning and meaning lurk beneath the luminous pictures; and the poem, besides being a description of the other world, and of the rewards and punishment meted out to souls, is a dramatic view of human passions in this life; a history of Italy and of the world; a theory of Church and State; the autobiography of an exile; and the confessions of a Christian, and of a lover, conscious of his sins and of the miracle of divine grace that intervenes to save him.

The subject-matter of the *Divine Comedy* is accordingly the moral universe in all its levels, — romantic, political, religious. To present these moral facts in a graphic way, the poet performed a double work of imagination. First he chose some historical personage that might plausibly illustrate each condition of the soul. Then he pictured this person in some characteristic and symbolic attitude of mind and of body, and in an appropriate, symbolic environment. To give material embodiment to moral ideas by such a method would nowadays be very artificial, and perhaps impossible; but in Dante's time everything was favourable to the attempt. We are accustomed to think of goods and evils as functions of a natural life, sparks struck out in the chance shock of men with things or with one another. For Dante, it was a matter of course that moral distinctions might be discerned, not merely as they arise incidentally in human experience, but also, and more genuinely, as they are displayed in the order of creation. The Creator himself was a poet producing allegories. The material world was a parable which he had built out in space, and ordered to be enacted. History was a great charade. The symbols of earthly poets are words or images; the symbols of the divine poet were natural things and the fortunes of men. They had been devised for a purpose; and this purpose, as the Koran, too, declares, had been precisely to show forth the great difference there is in God's sight between good and evil.

In Platonic cosmology, the concentric spheres were bodies formed and animated by intelligences of various orders. The nobler an intelligence, the more swift and outward, or higher, was the sphere it moved; whence the identification of "higher" with better, which survives, absurdly, to this day. And while Dante could not attribute literal truth to his fancies about hell, purgatory, and heaven, he believed that an actual heaven, purgatory, and hell had been fashioned by God on purpose to receive souls of varying deserts and complexion; so that while the poet's imagination, unless it reëchoed divine revelation, was only human and not prophetic, yet it was a genuine and plausible imagination, moving on the lines of nature, and anticipating such things as experience might very well realize. Dante's objectification of morality, his art of giving visible forms and local habitations to ideal virtues and vices, was for him a thoroughly serious and philosophical exercise. God had created nature and life on that very principle. The poet's method repeated the magic of Genesis. His symbolical imagination mirrored this symbolical world; it was a sincere anticipation of fact, no mere laboured and wilful allegory.

This situation has a curious consequence. Probably for the first and last time in the history of the world a classification worked out by a systematic moralist guided the vision of a great poet. Aristotle had distinguished, named, and classified the various virtues, with their opposites. But observe: if the other world was made on purpose—as it was—to express and render palpable those moral distinctions which were eternal, and to express and render them palpable in great detail, with all their possible tints and varieties; and if Aristotle had correctly classified moral qualities, as he had—then it follows that Aristotle (without knowing it) must have supplied the ground-plan, as it were, of hell and of heaven. Such was Dante's thought. With Aristotle's *Ethics* open

before him, with a supplementary hint, here and
there, drawn from the catechism, and with an ingrained preference (pious and almost philosophic) for
the number three and its multiples, he needed not to
voyage without a chart. The most visionary of subjects, life after death, could be treated with scientific soberness and deep sincerity. This vision was to
be no wanton dream. It was to be a sober meditation,
a philosophical prophecy, a probable drama,—the
most poignant, terrible, and consoling of all possible
truths.

The good—this was the fundamental thought of
Aristotle and of all Greek ethics,—the good is the
end at which nature aims. The demands of life cannot be radically perverse, since they are the judges of
every excellence. No man, as Dante says, could hate
his own soul; he could not at once be, and contradict,
the voice of his instincts and emotions. Nor could a
man hate God; for if that man knew himself, he
would see that God was, by definition, his natural
good, the ultimate goal of his actual aspirations.[1]
Since it was impossible, according to this insight,
that our faculties should be intrinsically evil, all evil

[1] *Purgatorio*, xvii. 106-11:

> Or perchè mai non può dalla salute
> Amor del suo suggetto volger viso,
> Dall' odio proprio son le cose tute:
> E perchè intender non si può diviso,
> E per sè stante, alcuno esser dal primo,
> Da quello odiare ogni affetto è deciso.

had to arise from the disorder into which these faculties fall, their too great weakness or strength in relation to one another. If the animal part of man was
too strong for his reason, he fell into incontinence,—
that is, into lust, gluttony, avarice, wrath, or pride.
Incontinence came from an excessive or ill-timed
pursuit of something good, of a part of what nature
aims at; for food, children, property, and character
are natural goods. These sins are accordingly the
most excusable and the least odious. Dante puts
those who have sinned through love in the first circle
of hell, nearest to the sunlight, or in the topmost
round of purgatory, nearest to the earthly paradise.
Below the lovers, in each case, are the gluttons,—
where a northern poet would have been obliged to
place his drunkards. Beneath these again are the
misers,—worse because less open to the excuse of
a merely childish lack of self-control.

The disorder of the faculties may arise, however,
in another way. The combative or spirited element,
rather than the senses, may get out of hand, and lead
to crimes of violence. Violence, like incontinence, is
spontaneous enough in its personal origin, and would
not be odious if it did not inflict, and intend to inflict. harm on others; so that besides incontinence,
there is malice in it. Ill-will to others may arise from
pride, because one loves to be superior to them, or

from envy, because one abhors that they should seem
superior to oneself; or through desire for vengeance,
because one smarts under some injury. Sins of these
kinds are more serious than those of foolish incontinence; they complicate the moral world more; they
introduce endless opposition of interests, and perpetual, self-propagating crimes. They are hateful.
Dante feels less pity for those who suffer by them:
he remembers the sufferings these malefactors have
themselves caused, and he feels a sort of joy in join-
ing the divine justice, and would gladly lash them
himself.

Worse still than violence, however, is guile: the
sin of those who in the service of their intemperance
or their malice have abused the gift of reason. *Cor-
ruptio optimi pessima;* and to turn reason, the faculty
that establishes order, into a means of organizing
disorder, is a perversity truly satanic: it turns evil
into an art. But even this perversity has stages; and
Dante distinguishes ten sorts of dishonesty or simple
fraud, as well as three sorts of treachery.

Besides these positive transgressions there is a possibility of general moral sluggishness and indifference. This Dante, with his fervid nature, particularly hates. He puts the Laodiceans in the fringe of
his hell; within the gate, that they may be without hope, but outside of limbo, that they may have

torments to endure, and be stung by wasps and hornets into a belated activity.[1]

To these vices, known to Aristotle, the Catholic moralist was obliged to add two others: original sin, of which spontaneous disbelief is one consequence, and heresy, or misbelief, after a revelation has been given and accepted. Original sin, and the paganism that goes with it, if they lead to nothing worse, are a mere privation of excellence and involve in eternity merely a privation of joy: they are punished in limbo. There sighs are heard, but no lamentation, and the only sorrow is to live in desire without hope. This fate is most appropriately imputed to the noble and clear-sighted in the hereafter, since it is so often their experience here. Dante was never juster than in this stroke.[2] Heresy, on the other hand, is a kind of

---

[1] *Inferno,* iii. 64–66:

> Questi sciaurati, che mai non fur vivi,
> Erano ignudi e stimolati molto
> Da mosconi e da vespe ch' erano ivi.

[2] *Ibid.,* iv. 41, 42:

> Semo perduti, e sol di tanto offesi
> Che senza speme vivemo in disio.

Cf. *Purgatorio,* iii. 37–45, where Virgil says:

> "State contenti, umana gente, al *quia;*
> Chè se potuto aveste veder tutto,
> Mestier non era partorir Maria;
> E disiar vedeste senza frutto
> Tai, che sarebbe lor disio quetato,
> Ch' eternalmente è dato lor per lutto.
> Io dico d' Aristotele e di Plato,
> E di molti altri." E qui chinò la fronte;
> E più non disse, e rimase turbato.

passion when honest, or a kind of fraud when politic;
and it is punished as pride in fiery tombs,[1] or as faction by perpetual gaping wounds and horrible muti-
lations.[2]

So far, with these slight additions, Dante is following Aristotle; but here a great divergence sets in. If
a pagan poet had conceived the idea of illustrating
the catalogue of vices and virtues in poetic scenes,
he would have chosen suitable episodes in human
life, and painted the typical characters that figured
in them in their earthly environment; for pagan morality is a plant of earth. Not so with Dante. His
poem describes this world merely in retrospect; the
foreground is occupied by the eternal consequences
of what time had brought forth. These consequences
are new facts, not merely, as for the rationalist, the
old facts conceived in their truth; they often reverse,
in their emotional quality, the events they represent. Such a reversal is made possible by the theory
that justice is partly retributive; that virtue is not
its own sufficient reward, nor vice its own sufficient
punishment. According to this theory, this life contains a part of our experience only, yet determines
the rest. The other life is a second experience, yet it
does not contain any novel adventures. It is deter-
mined altogether by what we have done on earth;

[1] *Inferno*, IX. 106–33, and X.
[2] *Ibid.*, XXVIII.

as the tree falleth so it lieth, and souls after death have no further initiative.

The theory Dante adopts mediates between two earlier views; in so far as it is Greek, it conceives immortality ideally, as something timeless; but in so far as it is Hebraic, it conceives of a new existence and a second, different taste of life. Dante thinks of a second experience, but of one that is wholly retrospective and changeless. It is an epilogue which sums up the play, and is the last episode in it. The purpose of this epilogue is not to carry on the play indefinitely: such a romantic notion of immortality never entered Dante's mind. The purpose of the epilogue is merely to vindicate (in a more unmistakable fashion than the play, being ill acted, itself could do) the excellence of goodness and the misery of vice. Were this life all, he thinks the wicked might laugh. If not wholly happy, at least they might boast that their lot was no worse than that of many good men. Nothing would make an overwhelming difference. Moral distinctions would be largely impertinent and remarkably jumbled. If I am a simple lover of goodness, I may perhaps put up with this situation. I may say of the excellences I prize what Wordsworth says of his Lucy: there may be none to praise and few to love them, but they make all the difference to me.

Dante, however, was not merely a simple lover of excellence: he was also a keen hater of wickedness,

one that took the moral world tragically and wished
to heighten the distinctions he felt into something
absolute and infinite. Now any man who is *enragé*
in his preferences will probably say, with Moham-
med, Tertullian, and Calvin, that good is dishonoured
if those who contemn it can go scot-free, and never
repent of their negligence; that the more horrible
the consequences of evil-doing, the more tolerable
the presence of evil-doing is in the world; and that
the everlasting shrieks and contortions of the damned
alone will make it possible for the saints to sit quiet,
and be convinced that there is perfect harmony in
the universe. On this principle, in the famous in-
scription which Dante places over the gate of hell,
we read that primal love, as well as justice and power,
established that torture-house; primal love, that is,
of that good which, by the extreme punishment of
those who scorn it, is honoured, vindicated, and made
to shine like the sun. The damned are damned for
the glory of God.

This doctrine, I cannot help thinking, is a great
disgrace to human nature. It shows how desperate,
at heart, is the folly of an egotistic or anthropocentric philosophy. This philosophy begins by assuring
us that everything is obviously created to serve our
needs; it then maintains that everything serves our
ideals; and in the end, it reveals that everything
serves our blind hatreds and superstitious qualms.

Because my instinct taboos something, the whole
universe, with insane intensity, shall taboo it for ever.
This infatuation was inherited by Dante, and it was
not uncongenial to his bitter and intemperate spleen.
Nevertheless, he saw beyond it at times. Like many
other Christian seers, he betrays here and there an
esoteric view of rewards and punishments, which
makes them simply symbols for the intrinsic quality
of good and evil ways. The punishment, he then
seems to say, is nothing added; it is what the passion
itself pursues; it is a fulfilment, horrifying the soul
that desired it.

For instance, spirits newly arrived in hell require
no devil with his prong to drive them to their punishment. They flit towards it eagerly, of their own
accord.[1] Similarly, the souls in purgatory are kept by
their own will at the penance they are doing. No
external force retains them, but until they are quite
purged they are not able, because they are not willing, to absolve themselves.[2] The whole mountain, we

[1] *Inferno*, III. 124–26:

> E pronti sono a trapassar lo rio,
> Chè la divina giustizia gli sprona
> Sì che la tema si volge in disio.

[2] *Purgatorio*, XXI. 61–69:

> Della mondizia sol voler fa prova,
> Che, tutta libera a mutar convento,
> L' alma sorprende, e di voler le giova....
> Ed io che son giaciuto a questa doglia
> Cinquecento anni e più, pur mo sentii
> Libera volontà di miglior soglia.

are told, trembles and bursts into psalmody when
any one frees himself and reaches heaven. Is it too
much of a gloss to say that these souls change their
prison when they change their ideal, and that an inferior state of soul is its own purgatory, and determines its own duration? In one place, at any rate,
Dante proclaims the intrinsic nature of punishment
in express terms. Among the blasphemers is a certain
king of Thebes, who defied the thunderbolts of Ju-
piter. He shows himself indifferent to his punishment
and says: "Such as I was alive, such I am dead."
Whereupon Virgil exclaims, with a force Dante had
never found in his voice before: "In that thy pride
is not mortified, thou art punished the more. No tor-
ture, other than thy own rage, would be woe enough
to match thy fury."[1] And indeed, Dante's imagination cannot outdo, it cannot even equal, the horrors
which men have brought upon themselves in this
world. If we were to choose the most fearful of the
scenes in the *Inferno*, we should have to choose the
story of Ugolino, but this is only a pale recital of
what Pisa had actually witnessed.

A more subtle and interesting instance, if a less
obvious one, may be found in the punishment of

[1] *Inferno*, xiv. 63–66:

> "O Capaneo, in ciò che non s' ammorza
> La tua superbia, se' tu più punito :
> Nullo martirio, fuor che la tua rabbia,
> Sarebbe al tuo furor dolor compito."

Paolo and Francesca di Rimini. What makes these
lovers so wretched in the Inferno? They are still together. Can an eternity of floating on the wind, in
each other's arms, be a punishment for lovers? That
is just what their passion, if left to speak for itself,
would have chosen. It is what passion stops at, and
would gladly prolong for ever. Divine judgement has
only taken it at its word. This fate is precisely what
Aucassin, in the well-known tale, wishes for himself
and his sweetheart Nicolette,—not a heaven to be
won by renunciation, but the possession, even if it
be in hell, of what he loves and fancies. And a great
romantic poet, Alfred de Musset, actually upbraids
Dante for not seeing that such an eternal destiny as
he has assigned to Paolo and Francesca would be
not the ruin of their love,[1] but the perfect fulfilment
of it. This last seems to be very true; but did Dante
overlook the truth of it? If so, what instinct guided

---

[1] Alfred de Musset, *Poésies Nouvelles, Souvenir:*

> Dante, pourquoi dis-tu qu'il n'est pire misère
> Qu'un souvenir heureux dans les jours de douleur?
> Quel chagrin t'a dicté cette parole amère,
>   Cette offense au malheur?
>
> . . . Ce blasphème vanté ne vient pas de ton cœur.
> Un souvenir heureux est peut-être sur terre
>   Plus vrai que le bonheur. . . .
>
> Et c'est à ta Françoise, à ton ange de gloire,
> Que tu pouvais donner ces mots à prononcer,
> Elle qui s'interrompt, pour conter son histoire,
>   D'un eternel baiser !

him to choose just the fate for these lovers that they
would have chosen for themselves?

There is a great difference between the apprentices in life, and the masters,—Aucassin and Alfred
de Musset were among the apprentices; Dante was
one of the masters. He could feel the fresh promptings of life as keenly as any youngster, or any romanticist; but he had lived these things through, he
knew the possible and the impossible issue of them;
he saw their relation to the rest of human nature,
and to the ideal of an ultimate happiness and peace.
He had discovered the necessity of saying continually to oneself: Thou shalt renounce. And for this
reason he needed no other furniture for hell than
the literal ideals and fulfilments of our absolute little
passions. The soul that is possessed by any one of
these passions nevertheless has other hopes in abey-
ance. Love itself dreams of more than mere possession; to conceive happiness, it must conceive a life
to be shared in a varied world, full of events and
activities, which shall be new and ideal bonds between the lovers. But unlawful love cannot pass out
into this public fulfilment. It is condemned to be
mere possession—possession in the dark, without an
environment, without a future. It is love among the
ruins. And it is precisely this that is the torment of
Paolo and Francesca—love among the ruins of themselves and of all else they might have had to give to

one another. Abandon yourself, Dante would say to us,—abandon yourself altogether to a love that is nothing but love, and you are in hell already. Only an inspired poet could be so subtle a moralist. Only a sound moralist could be so tragic a poet.

The same tact and fine feeling that appear in these little moral dramas appear also in the sympathetic landscape in which each episode is set. The poet actually accomplishes the feat which he attributes to the Creator; he evokes a material world to be the fit theatre for moral attitudes. Popular imagination and the precedents of Homer and Virgil had indeed carried him halfway in this symbolic labour, as tradition almost always carries a poet who is successful. Mankind, from remotest antiquity, had conceived a dark subterranean hell, inhabited by unhappy ghosts. In Christian times, these shades had become lost souls, tormented by hideous demons. But Dante, with the Aristotelian chart of the vices before him, turned those vague windy caverns into a symmetrical labyrinth. Seven concentric terraces descended, step by step, towards the waters of the Styx, which in turn encircled the brazen walls of the City of Dis, or Pluto. Within these walls, two more terraces led down to the edge of a prodigious precipice —perhaps a thousand miles deep—which formed the pit of hell. At the bottom of this, still sinking gently towards the centre, were ten concentric furrows or ditches, to hold ten sorts of rogues; and finally a last sheer precipice fell to the frozen lake of Cocytus, at the very centre of the earth, in the midst of which Lucifer was congealed amongst lesser traitors.

Precision and horror, graphic and moral truth, were never so wonderfully combined as in the description of this hell. Yet the conception of purgatory is more original, and perhaps more poetical. The very approach to the place is enchanting. We hear of it first in the fatal adventure ascribed to Ulysses by Dante. Restless at Ithaca after his return from Troy, the hero had summoned his surviving companions for a last voyage of discovery. He had sailed with them past the Pillars of Hercules, skirting the African shore; until after three months of open sea, he saw a colossal mountain, a great truncated cone, looming before him. This was the island and hill of purgatory, at the very antipodes of Jerusalem. Yet before Ulysses could land there, a squall overtook him; and his galley sank, prow foremost, in that untraversed sea, within sight of a new world. So must the heathen fail of salvation, though some oracular impulse bring them near the goal.

How easy is success, on the other hand, to the ministers of grace! From the mouth of the Tiber, where the souls of Christians congregate after death, a light skiff, piloted by an angel, and propelled only by his white wings, skims the sea swiftly towards the mountain of purgatory, there deposits the spirits it carries, and is back at the mouth of the Tiber again on the same day. So much for the approach to purgatory. When a spirit lands it finds the skirts of the mountain broad and spreading, but the slope soon becomes hard and precipitous. When he has passed the narrow gate of repentance, he must stay upon each of the ledges that encircle the mountain at various heights, until one of his sins is purged, and then upon the next ledge above, if he has been guilty also of the sin that is atoned for there. The mountain is so high as to lift its head into the sphere of the moon, above the reach of terrestrial tempests. The top, which is a broad circular plain, contains the Garden of Eden, watered by the rivers Lethe and Eunoe, one to heal all painful memories, and the other to bring all good thoughts to clearness. From this place, which literally touches the lowest heaven, the upward flight is easy from sphere to sphere.

The astronomy of Dante's day fell in beautifully with his poetic task. It described and measured a firmament that would still be identified with the posthumous heaven of the saints. The whirling invisible spheres of that astronomy had the earth for their centre. The sublime complexities of this Ptolemaic system were day and night before Dante's mind. He loves to tell us in what constellation the sun is rising or setting, and what portion of the sky is then over the antipodes; he carries in his mind an orrery that shows him, at any given moment, the position of every star.

Such a constant dragging in of astronomical lore may seem to us puerile or pedantic; but for Dante the astronomical situation had the charm of a landscape, literally full of the most wonderful lights and shadows; and it also had the charm of a hard-won discovery that unveiled the secrets of nature. To think straight, to see things as they are, or as they might naturally be, interested him more than to fancy things impossible; and in this he shows, not want of imagination, but true imaginative power and imaginative maturity. It is those of us who are too feeble to conceive and master the real world, or too cowardly to face it, that run away from it to those cheap fictions that alone seem to us fine enough for poetry or for religion. In Dante the fancy is not empty or arbitrary; it is serious, fed on the study of real things. It adopts their tendency and divines their true destiny. His art is, in the original Greek sense, an imitation or rehearsal of nature, an anticipation of fate. For this reason curious details of science or theology enter as a matter of course into his verse. With the straightforward faith and simplicity of his age he devours these interesting images, which help him to clarify the mysteries of this world.

There is a kind of sensualism or aestheticism that

has decreed in our day that theory is not poetical; as if all the images and emotions that enter a cultivated mind were not saturated with theory. The prevalence of such a sensualism or aestheticism would alone suffice to explain the impotence of the arts. The life of theory is not less human or less emotional than the life of sense; it is more typically human and more keenly emotional. Philosophy is a more intense sort of experience than common life is, just as pure and subtle music, heard in retirement, is something keener and more intense than the howling of storms or the rumble of cities. For this reason philosophy, when a poet is not mindless, enters inevitably into his poetry, since it has entered into his life; or rather, the detail of things and the detail of ideas pass equally into his verse, when both alike lie in the path that has led him to his ideal. To object to theory in poetry would be like objecting to words there; for words, too, are symbols without the sensuous character of the things they stand for; and yet it is only by the net of new connections which words throw over things, in recalling them, that poetry arises at all. Poetry is an attenuation, a rehandling, an echo of crude experience; it is itself a theoretic vision of things at arm's length.

Never before or since has a poet lived in so large a landscape as Dante; for our infinite times and distances are of little poetic value while we have no graphic image of what may fill them. Dante's spaces were filled; they enlarged, to the limits of human imagination, the habitations and destinies of mankind. Although the saints did not literally inhabit the spheres, but the empyrean beyond, yet each spirit could be manifested in that sphere the genius of which was most akin to his own. In Dante's vision spirits appear as points of light, from which voices also flow sometimes, as well as radiance. Further than reporting their words (which are usually about the things of earth) Dante tells us little about them. He has indeed, at the end, a vision of a celestial rose; tier upon tier of saints are seated as in an amphitheatre, and the Deity overarches them in the form of a triple rainbow, with a semblance of man in the midst. But this is avowedly a mere symbol, a somewhat conventional picture to which Dante has recourse unwillingly, for want of a better image to render his mystical intention. What may perhaps help us to divine this intention is the fact, just mentioned, that according to him the celestial spheres are not the real seat of any human soul; that the pure rise through them with increasing ease and velocity, the nearer they come to God; and that the eyes of Beatrice—the revelation of God to man— are only mirrors, shedding merely reflected beauty and light.

These hints suggest the doctrine that the goal of

life is the very bosom of God; not any finite form of existence, however excellent, but a complete absorption and disappearance in the Godhead. So the Neoplatonists had thought, from whom all this heavenly landscape is borrowed; and the reservations that Christian orthodoxy requires have not always remained present to the minds of Christian mystics and poets. Dante broaches this very point in the memorable interview he has with the spirit of Piccarda, in the third canto of the *Paradiso*. She is in the lowest sphere of heaven, that of the inconstant moon, because after she had been stolen from her convent and forcibly married, she felt no prompting to renew her earlier vows. Dante asks her if she never longs for a higher station in paradise, one nearer to God, the natural goal of all aspiration. She answers that to share the will of God, who has established many different mansions in his house, is to be truly one with him. The wish to be nearer God would actually carry the soul farther away, since it would oppose the order he has established.[1]

---

[1] *Paradiso*, III. 73–90:

> "Se disiassimo esser più superne,
>   Foran discordi li nostri disiri
>   Dal voler di colui che qui ne cerne, . . .
> E la sua volontate è nostra pace;
>   Ella è quel mare al qual tutto si move
>   Ciò ch' ella crea, e che natura face."
> Chiaro mi fu allor com' ogni dove
>   In cielo è Paradiso, e sì la grazia
>   Del sommo ben d' un modo non vi piove.

Even in heaven, therefore, the Christian saint was
to keep his essential fidelity, separation, and lowli-
ness. He was to feel still helpless and lost in himself,
like Tobias, and happy only in that the angel of the
Lord was holding him by the hand. For Piccarda
to say that she accepts the will of God means not
that she shares it, but that she submits to it. She
would fain go higher, for her moral nature demands
it, as Dante—incorrigible Platonist—perfectly perceived; but she dare not mention it, for she knows
that God, whose thoughts are not her thoughts, has
forbidden it. The inconstant sphere of the moon does
not afford her a perfect happiness; but, chastened as
she is, she says it brings her happiness enough; all
that a broken and a contrite heart has the courage
to hope for.

Such are the conflicting inspirations beneath the
lovely harmonies of the *Paradiso*. It was not the
poet's soul that was in conflict here; it was only his
traditions. The conflicts of his own spirit had been
left behind in other regions; on that threshing-floor
of earth which, from the height of heaven, he looked
back upon with wonder,[1] surprised that men should

---

[1] *Paradiso*, xxii. 133–39 :

> Col viso ritornai per tutte e quante
>   Le sette spere, e vidi questo globo
>   Tal, ch' io sorrisi del suo vil sembiante ;
> E quel consiglio per migliore approbo
>   Che l' ha per meno ; e chi ad altro pensa
>   Chiamar si puote veramente probo.

take so passionately this trouble of ants, which he judges best, says Dante, who thinks least of it.

In this saying the poet is perhaps conscious of a personal fault; for Dante was far from perfect, even as a poet. He was too much a man of his own time, and often wrote with a passion not clarified into judgement. So much does the purely personal and dramatic interest dominate us as we read of a Boniface or an Ugolino that we forget that these historical figures are supposed to have been transmuted into the eternal, and to have become bits in the mosaic of Platonic essences. Dante himself almost forgets it. The modern reader, accustomed to insignificant, wayward fictions, and expecting to be entertained by images without thoughts, may not notice this lack of perspective, or may rejoice in it. But, if he is judicious, he will not rejoice in it long. The Bonifaces and the Ugolinos are not the truly deep, the truly lovely figures of the *Divine Comedy*. They are, in a relative sense, the vulgarities in it. We feel too much, in these cases, the heat of the poet's prejudice or indignation. He is not just, as he usually is; he does not stop to think, as he almost always does. He forgets that he is in the eternal world, and dips for the moment into a brawl in some Italian market-place, or into the council-chamber of some factious *condottiere*. The passages—such as those about Boniface and Ugolino—which Dante writes in this mood are powerful and vehement, but they are not beautiful. They brand the object of their invective more than they reveal it; they shock more than they move the reader.

This lower kind of success—for it is still a success in rhetoric—falls to the poet because he has abandoned the Platonic half of his inspiration and has become for the moment wholly historical, wholly Hebraic or Roman. He would have been a far inferior mind if he had always moved on this level. With the Platonic spheres and the Aristotelian ethics taken out, his *Comedy* would not have been divine. Persons and incidents, to be truly memorable, have to be rendered significant; they have to be seen in their place in the moral world; they have to be judged, and judged rightly, in their dignity and value. A casual personal sentiment towards them, however passionate, cannot take the place of the sympathetic insight that comprehends and the wide experience that judges.

Again (what is fundamental with Dante) love, as he feels and renders it, is not normal or healthy love. It was doubtless real enough, but too much restrained and expressed too much in fancy; so that when it is extended Platonically and identified so easily with the grace of God and with revealed wisdom, we feel the suspicion that if the love in question had been natural and manly it would have offered more resistance to so mystical a transformation. The poet who wishes to pass convincingly from love to philosophy (and that seems a natural progress for a poet) should accordingly be a hearty and complete lover—a lover like Goethe and his Faust—rather than like Plato and Dante. Faust, too, passes from Gretchen to Helen, and partly back again; and Goethe made even more passages. Had any of them led to something which not only was loved, but deserved to be loved, which not only could inspire a whole life, but which ought to inspire it—then we should have had a genuine progress.

In the next place, Dante talks too much about himself. There is a sense in which this egotism is a merit, or at least a ground of interest for us moderns; for egotism is the distinctive attitude of modern philosophy and of romantic sentiment. In being egotistical Dante was ahead of his time. His philosophy would have lost an element of depth, and his poetry an element of pathos, had he not placed himself in the centre of the stage, and described everything as his experience, or as a revelation made to himself and made for the sake of his personal salvation. But Dante's egotism goes rather further than was requisite, so that the transcendental insight might not fail in his philosophy. It extended so far that he cast the shadow of his person not only over the terraces of purgatory (as he is careful to tell us repeatedly), but over the whole of Italy and of Europe, which he saw and judged under the evident influence of private passions and resentments.

Moreover, the personality thrust forward so obtrusively is not in every respect worthy of contemplation. Dante is very proud and very bitter; at the same time, he is curiously timid; and one may tire sometimes of his perpetual tremblings and tears, of his fainting fits and his intricate doubts. A man who knows he is under the special protection of God, and of three celestial ladies, and who has such a sage and magician as Virgil for a guide, might have looked even upon hell with a little more confidence. How far is this shivering and swooning philosopher from the laughing courage of Faust, who sees his poodle swell into a monster, then into a cloud, and finally change into Mephistopheles, and says at once: *Das also war des Pudels Kern!* Doubtless Dante was mediaeval, and contrition, humility, and fear of the devil were great virtues in those days; but the conclusion we must come to is precisely that the virtues of those days were not the best virtues, and that a poet who represents that time cannot be a fair nor an ultimate spokesman for humanity.

Perhaps we have now reviewed the chief objects that peopled Dante's imagination, the chief objects into the midst of which his poetry transports us; and if a poet's genius avails to transport us into his enchanted world, the character of that world will determine the quality and dignity of his poetry. Dante transports us, with unmistakable power, first into the atmosphere of a visionary love; then into the history of his conversion, affected by this love, or by the divine grace identified with it. The supreme ideal to which his conversion brought him back is expressed for him by universal nature, and is embodied among men in the double institution of a revealed religion and a providential empire. To trace the fortunes of these institutions, we are transported next into the panorama of history, in its great crises and its great men; and particularly into the panorama of Italy in the poet's time, where we survey the crimes, the virtues, and the sorrows of those prominent in furthering or thwarting the ideal of Christendom. These numerous persons are set before us with the sympathy and brevity of a dramatist; yet it is no mere carnival, no *danse macabre:* for throughout, above the confused strife of parties and passions, we hear the steady voice, the implacable sentence, of the prophet that judges them.

Thus Dante, gifted with the tenderest sense of colour, and the firmest art of design, has put his whole world into his canvas. Seen there, that world becomes complete, clear, beautiful, and tragic. It is vivid and truthful in its detail, sublime in its march and in its harmony. This is not poetry where the parts are better than the whole. Here, as in some great symphony, everything is cumulative: the movements conspire, the tension grows, the volume redoubles, the keen melody soars higher and higher; and it all ends, not with a bang, not with some casual incident, but in sustained reflection, in the sense that it has not ended, but remains by us in its totality, a revelation and a resource for ever. It has taught us to love and to renounce, to judge and to worship. What more could a poet do? Dante poetized all life and nature as he found them. His imagination dominated and focused the whole world. He thereby touched the ultimate goal to which a poet can aspire; he set the standard for all possible performance, and became the type of a supreme poet. This is not to say that he is the "greatest" of poets. The relative merit of poets is a barren thing to wrangle about. The question can always be opened anew, when a critic appears with a fresh temperament or a new criterion. Even less need we say that no greater poet can ever arise; we may be confident of the opposite. But Dante gives a successful example of the *highest species* of poetry. His poetry covers the whole field from which poetry may be fetched, and to which poetry may be applied, from the inmost recesses of the heart to the uttermost bounds of nature and of destiny. If to give imaginative value to something is the minimum task of a poet, to give imaginative value to all things, and to the system which things compose, is evidently his greatest task.

Dante fulfilled this task, of course under special conditions and limitations, personal and social; but he fulfilled it, and he thereby fulfilled the conditions of supreme poetry. Even Homer, as we are beginning to perceive nowadays, suffered from a certain conventionality and one-sidedness. There was much in the life and religion of his time that his art ignored. It was a flattering, a euphemistic art; it had a sort of pervasive blandness, like that which we now associate with a fashionable sermon. It was poetry addressed to the ruling caste in the state, to the conquerors; and it spread an intentional glamour over their past brutalities and present self-deceptions. No such partiality in Dante; he paints what he hates as frankly as what he loves, and in all things he is complete and sincere. If any similar adequacy is attained again by any poet, it will not be, presumably, by a poet of the supernatural. Henceforth, for any wide and honest imagination, the supernatural must figure as an idea in the human mind,—a part of the natural. To conceive it otherwise would be to fall short of the insight of this age, not to express or to complete it. Dante, however, for this very reason, may be expected to remain the supreme poet of the supernatural, the unrivalled exponent, after Plato, of that phase of thought and feeling in which the supernatural seems to be the key to nature and to happiness. This is the hypothesis on which, as yet, moral unity has been best attained in this world. Here, then, we have the most complete idealization and comprehension of things achieved by mankind hitherto. Dante is the type of a consummate poet.

GOETHE'S FAUST

IV

GOETHE'S FAUST

IN approaching the third of our philosophical poets, there is a scruple that may cross the mind. Lucretius was undoubtedly a philosophical poet; his whole poem is devoted to expounding and defending a system of philosophy. In Dante the case is almost as plain. The *Divine Comedy* is a moral and personal fable; yet not only are many passages explicitly philosophical, but the whole is inspired and controlled by the most definite of religious systems and of moral codes. Dante, too, is unmistakably a philosophical poet. But was Goethe a philosopher? And is *Faust* a philosophical poem?

If we say so, it must be by giving a certain latitude to our terms. Goethe was the wisest of mankind; too wise, perhaps, to be a philosopher in the technical sense, or to try to harness this wild world in a brain-spun terminology. It is true that he was all his life a follower of Spinoza, and that he may be termed, without hesitation, a naturalist in philosophy and a pantheist. His adherence to the general attitude of Spinoza, however, did not exclude a great plasticity and freedom in his own views, even on the most fundamental points. Thus Goethe did not admit the mechanical interpretation of nature advocated by Spinoza. He also assigned, at least to privileged souls, like his own, a more personal sort of immortality than Spinoza allowed. Moreover, he harboured a generous sympathy with the dramatic explanations of nature and history current in the Germany of his day. Yet such transcendental idealism, making the world the expression of a spiritual endeavour, was a total reversal of that conviction, so profound in Spinoza, that all moral energies are resident in particular creatures, themselves sparks in an absolutely infinite and purposeless world. In a word, Goethe was not a systematic philosopher. His feeling for the march of things and for the significance of great personages and great ideas was indeed philosophical, although more romantic than scientific. His thoughts upon life were fresh and miscellaneous. They voiced the genius and learning of his age. They did not express a firm personal attitude, radical and unified, and transmissible to other times and persons. For philosophers, after all, have this advantage over men of letters, that their minds, being more organic, can more easily propagate themselves. They scatter less influence, but more seeds.

If from Goethe we turn to *Faust*—and it is as the author of *Faust* only that we shall consider him— the situation is not less ambiguous. In the play, as the young Goethe first wrote it, philosophy appeared in the first line,—*Hab nun ach die Philosophey;* but it appeared there, and throughout the piece, merely

as a human experience, a passion or an illusion, a fund
of images or an ambitious art. Later, it is true, under
the spell of fashion and of Schiller, Goethe surrounded his original scenes with others, like the prologue in heaven, or the apotheosis of Faust, in which
a philosophy of life was indicated; namely, that he
who strives strays, yet in that straying finds his
salvation. This idea left standing all that satirical
and Mephistophelian wisdom with which the whole
poem abounds, the later parts no less than the earlier.
Frankly, it was a moral that adorned the tale, without having been the seed of it, and without even expressing fairly the spirit which it breathes. *Faust* remained an essentially romantic poem, written to give
vent to a pregnant and vivid genius, to touch the
heart, to bewilder the mind with a carnival of images,
to amuse, to thrill, to humanize; and, if we must
speak of philosophy, there were many express maxims in the poem, and many insights, half betrayed,
that exceeded in philosophic value the belated and
official moral which the author affixed to it, and which
he himself warned us not to take too seriously.[1]

Faust is, then, no philosophical poem, after an
open or deliberate fashion; and yet it offers a solution to the moral problem of existence as truly as

---

[1] Eckermann, Conversation of May 6, 1827 : "Das ist zwar ein wirksamer,
manches erklärender, guter Gedanke, aber es ist keine Idee die dem Gan-
zen . . . zugrunde liege."

do the poems of Lucretius and Dante. Heard philosophies are sweet, but those unheard may be sweeter.
They may be more unmixed and more profound for
being adopted unconsciously, for being lived rather
than taught. This is not merely to say what might
be said of every work of art and of every natural
object, that it could be made the starting-point for
a chain of inferences that should reveal the whole
universe, like the flower in the crannied wall. It
is to say, rather, that the vital straining towards an
ideal, definite but latent, when it dominates a whole
life, may express that ideal more fully than could
the best-chosen words.

Now *Faust* is the foam on the top of two great
waves of human aspiration, merging and heaping
themselves up together,—the wave of romanticism
rising from the depths of northern traditions and
genius, and the wave of a new paganism coming
from Greece over Italy. These are not philosophies
to be read into *Faust* by the critic; they are passions seething in the drama. It is the drama of a
philosophical adventure; a rebellion against convention; a flight to nature, to tenderness, to beauty;
and then a return to convention again, with a feeling that nature, tenderness, and beauty, unless found
there, will not be found at all. Goethe never depicts,
as Dante does, the object his hero is pursuing; he is
satisfied with depicting the pursuit. Like Lessing, in

his famous apologue, he prefers the pursuit of the ideal to the ideal itself; perhaps, as in the case of Lessing, because the hope of realizing the ideal, and the interest in realizing it, were beginning to forsake him.

The case is somewhat as that of Dante would have been if, instead of recognizing and loving Beatrice at first sight and rising into a vision of the eternal world, ready-made and perfectly ordered, Dante had passed from love to love, from *donna gentile* to *donna gentile*, always longing for the eyes of Beatrice without ever meeting them. The *Divine Comedy* would then have been only human, yet it might have suggested and required the very consummation that the *Divine Comedy* depicts; and without expressing this consummation, our human comedy might have furnished materials and momentum for it, such that, if ever that consummation came to be expressed, it would be more deeply felt and more adequately understood. Dante gives us a philosophical goal, and we have to recall and retrace the journey; Goethe gives us a philosophic journey, and we have to divine the goal.

Goethe is a romantic poet; he is a novelist in verse. He is a philosopher of experience as it comes to the individual; the philosopher of life, as action, memory, or soliloquy may put life before each of us in turn. Now the zest of romanticism consists in

taking what you know is an independent and ancient
world as if it were material for your private emotions. The savage or the animal, who should not be
aware of nature or history at all, could not be romantic about them, nor about himself. He would be
blandly idiotic, and take everything quite unsuspect-
ingly for what it was in him. The romanticist, then,
should be a civilized man, so that his primitiveness
and egotism may have something paradoxical and
conscious about them; and so that his life may contain a rich experience, and his reflection may play
with all varieties of sentiment and thought. At the
same time, in his inmost genius, he should be a
barbarian, a child, a transcendentalist, so that his life
may seem to him absolutely fresh, self-determined,
unforeseen, and unforeseeable. It is part of his inspiration to believe that he creates a new heaven
and a new earth with each revolution in his moods
or in his purposes. He ignores, or seeks to ignore,
all the conditions of life, until perhaps by living he
personally discovers them.[1] Like Faust, he flouts science, and is minded to make trial of magic, which

---

[1] *Faust*, Part ii. Act v. 375-82:

> Ich bin nur durch die Welt gerannt;
> Ein jed' Gelüst ergriff ich bei den Haaren,
> Was nicht genügte, liess ich fahren,
> Was mir entwischte, liess ich ziehn.
> Ich habe nur begehrt und nur vollbracht
> Und abermals gewünscht und so mit Macht
> Mein Leben durchgestürmt; erst gross und mächtig,
> Nun aber geht es weise, geht bedächtig.

renders a man's will master of the universe in which
he seems to live. He disowns all authority, save that
mysteriously exercised over him by his deep faith
in himself. He is always honest and brave; but he is
always different, and absolves himself from his past
as soon as he has outgrown or forgotten it. He is
inclined to be wayward and foolhardy, justifying
himself on the ground that all experience is interesting, that the springs of it are inexhaustible and always
pure, and that the future of his soul is infinite. In
the romantic hero the civilized man and the barbarian must be combined; he should be the heir to all
civilization, and, nevertheless, he should take life
arrogantly and egotistically, as if it were an absolute
personal experiment.

   This singular combination was strikingly exem-
plified in Doctor Johannes Faustus, a figure half
historical, half legendary, familiar to Goethe in his
boyhood in puppet-shows and chapbooks. An ad-
venturer in the romantic as well as in the vulgar
sense of the word, somewhat like Paracelsus or Giordano Bruno, Doctor Faustus had felt the mystery
of nature, had scorned authority, had credited magic,
had lived by imposture, and had fled from the po-
lice. His blasphemous boasts and rascally conduct,
together with his magic arts, had made him even in
his lifetime a scandalous and interesting personage.
He was scarcely dead when legends gathered about

his name. It was published abroad that he had sold his soul to the devil, in exchange for twenty-four years of wild pleasures upon earth.

This legend purported to offer a terrible and edifying example, a warning to all Christians to avoid the snares of science, of pleasure, and of ambition. These things had sent Doctor Faustus into hell-fire; his corpse, found face downward, could not be turned over upon its back. Nevertheless, we may suspect that even at the beginning people recognized in Doctor Faustus a braver brother, a somewhat enviable reprobate who had dared to relish the good things of this life above the sad joys vaguely promised for the other. All that the Renaissance valued was here represented as in the devil's gift; and the man in the street might well doubt whether it was religion or worldly life that was thereby made the more unlovely. Doubtless the Lutheran authors of the first chapbook felt, and felt rightly, that those fine things which tempted Faustus were unevangelical, pagan, and popish; yet they could not cease altogether to admire and even to covet them, especially when the first ardours of the Old-Christian revival had had time to cool.

Marlowe, who wrote only a few years later, made a beginning in the rehabilitation of the hero. His Faustus is still damned, but he is transformed into the sort of personage that Aristotle approves of for the hero of tragedy, essentially human and noble, but led astray by some excusable vice or error. Marlowe's public would see in Doctor Faustus a man and a Christian like themselves, carried a bit too far by ambition and the love of pleasure. He is no radical unbeliever, no natural mate for the devil, conscienceless and heathen, like the typical villain of the Renaissance. On the contrary, he has become a good Protestant, and holds manfully to all those parts of the creed which express his spontaneous affections. A good angel is often overheard whispering in his ear; and if the bad angel finally prevails, it is in spite of continual remorse and hesitation on the Doctor's part. This excellent Faustus is damned by accident or by predestination; he is brow-beaten by the devil and forbidden to repent when he has really repented. The terror of the conclusion is thereby heightened; we see an essentially good man, because in a moment of infatuation he had signed away his soul, driven against his will to despair and damnation. The alternative of a happy solution lies almost at hand; and it is only a lingering taste for the lurid and the horrible, ingrained in this sort of melodrama, that sends him shrieking to hell.

What makes Marlowe's conclusion the more violent and the more unphilosophical is the fact that, to any one not dominated by convention, the good angel, in the dialogue, seems to have so much the worse of the argument. All he has to offer is sour admonition and external warnings:

> O Faustus, lay that damnèd book aside,
> And gaze not on it lest it tempt thy soul,
> And heap God's heavy wrath upon thy head.
> Read, read, the Scriptures; that is blasphemy. . . .
> Sweet Faustus, think of heaven, and heavenly things.

To which the evil angel replies:

> No, Faustus, think of honour and of wealth.

And in another place:

> Go forward, Faustus, in that famous art,
> Wherein all nature's treasure is contained.
> Be thou on earth as Jove is in the sky,
> Lord and commander of these elements.

There can be no doubt that the devil here represents the natural ideal of Faustus, or of any child of the Renaissance; he appeals to the vague but healthy ambitions of a young soul, that would make trial of the world. In other words, this devil represents the true good, and it is no wonder if the honest Faustus cannot resist his suggestions. We like him for his love of life, for his trust in nature, for his enthusiasm for beauty. He speaks for us all when he cries:

> Was this the face that launched a thousand ships
> And burnt the topless towers of Ilium?

Even his irreverent pranks, being directed against the pope, endear him the more to an anti-clerical public; and he appeals to courtiers and cavaliers by his lofty poetical scorn for such crabbed professions as the law, medicine, or theology. In a word, Marlowe's Faustus is a martyr to everything that the Renaissance prized,—power, curious knowledge, enterprise, wealth, and beauty.

How thoroughly Marlowe and Goethe are on the way towards reversing the Christian philosophy of life may be seen if we compare *Faust* for a moment (as, in other respects, has often been done) with *The Wonder-working Magician* of Calderon. This earlier hero, St. Cyprian of Antioch, is like Faust in being a scholar, signing away his soul to the devil, practising magic, embracing the ghost of beauty, and being ultimately saved. Here the analogy ends. Cyprian, far from being disgusted with all theory, and particularly with theology, is a pagan philosopher eagerly seeking God, and working his way, with full faith in his method, toward Christian orthodoxy. He floors the devil in scholastic argument about the unity of God, his power, wisdom, and goodness. He falls in love, and sells his soul merely in the hope of satisfying his passion. He studies magic chiefly for the same reason; but magic cannot overrule the free-will of the Christian lady he loves (a modern and very Spanish one, though supposed to adorn ancient Antioch). The devil can supply only a false phantasm of her person, and as Cyprian approaches her and lifts her veil, he finds a hideous death's-head beneath; for God can work miracles to cap those of any magician, and can beat the devil at his own game. Thunderstruck at this portent, Cyprian becomes a Christian. Half-naked, ecstatic, taken for a madman, he bears witness loudly and persistently to the power, wisdom, and goodness of the one true God; and, since the persecution of Decius is then going on, he is hurried away to martyrdom. His lady, sentenced also for the same cause, encourages him by her heroic attitude and words. Their earthly passion is dead; but their souls are united in death and in immortality.

In this drama we see magic checkmated by miracles, doubt yielding to faith, purity resisting temptation, passion transformed into zeal, and all the glories of the world collapsing before disillusion and asceticism. These glories are nothing, the poet tells us, but dust, ashes, smoke, and air.

The contrast with Goethe's *Faust* could not be more complete. Both poets take the greatest liberties with their chronology, yet the spirit of their dramas is remarkably true to the respective ages in which they are supposed to occur. Calderon glorifies the movement from paganism to Christianity. The philosophy in which that movement culminated— Catholic orthodoxy—still dominates the poet's mind, not in a perfunctory way, but so as to kindle his imagination, and render his personages sublime and his verses rapturous. Goethe's *Faust*, on the contrary, glorifies the return from Christianity to paganism. It shows the spirit of the Renaissance liberating the soul, and bursting the bonds of traditional faith and traditional morals. This spirit, after manifesting itself brilliantly at the time of the historical Faust, had seemed to be smothered in the great world during the seventeenth century. Men's characters and laws had reaffirmed their old allegiance to Christianity, and the Renaissance survived only abstractly, in scholarship or the fine arts, to which it continued to lend a certain classic or pseudo-classic elegance. In Goethe's time, however, a second Renaissance was taking place in the souls of men. The love of life, primal and adventurous, was gathering head in many an individual. In the romantic movement and in the French Revolution, this love of life freed itself from the politic compromises and conventions that had been stifling it for two hundred years. Goethe's hero embodies this second, romantic emancipation of the mind, too long an unwilling pupil of Christian tradition. He cries for air, for nature, for all experience. Cyprian, on the other hand, an unwilling pupil of paganism, had yearned for truth, for solitude, and for heaven.

Such was the legend that, to the great good fortune of mankind, fascinated the young Goethe, and took root in his fancy. Around it gathered the ex-

periences and insights of sixty well-filled years: *Faust*
became the poetical autobiography and the philosophic testament of Goethe. He stuffed it with every
enthusiasm that diversified his own life, from the
great alternative of romantic or classical art, down
to the controversy between Neptunism and Vulcan-
ism in geology, and to his fatherly admiration for
Lord Byron. Yet in spite of the liberties he took with
the legend, and the personal turn he gave it, nothing
in its historical associations escaped him. His life
in Frankfort and in Strassburg had made the mediaeval scene familiar to his fancy; Herder had com-
municated to him an imaginative cult for all that
was national and characteristic in art and manners;
the spell of Gothic architecture had fallen on him;
and he had learned to feel in Shakespeare the infinite
strength of suggestion in details, in multitudinous
glimpses, in lifelike medleys of sadness and mirth, in
a humble realism in externals, amid lyric and metaphysical outpourings of the passions. The sense for
classic beauty which had inspired Marlowe with immortal lines, and was later to inspire his own *Helena*,
was as yet dormant; but instead he had caught the
humanitarian craze, then prevalent, for defending and
idealizing the victims of law and society, among
others, the poor girl who, to escape disgrace, did away
with her new-born child. Such a victim of a selfish
seducer and a Pharisaical public was to add a de-

sirable touch of femininity and pathos to the story of
Faust: Gretchen was to take the place, at least for
the nonce, of the coveted Helen.

This Gretchen was to be no common creature, but
one endowed with all the innocence, sweetness, intelligence, fire, and fortitude which Goethe was finding, or thought he was finding, in his own Gretchens,
Kätchens, and Frederickes. For the young Goethe,
though very learned, was no mere student of books;
to his human competence and power to succeed,
he joined the gusts of feeling, the irresponsible raptures, the sudden sorrows, of a genuine poet. He was
a true lover, and a wayward one. He could delve
into magic with awe, in a Faust-like spirit of adventure; he could burn offerings in his attic to the
rising sun; he could plunge into Christian mysticism;
and there could well up, on occasion, from the deep
store of his unconscious mind, floods of words, of
images, and of tears. He was a genius, if ever there
was one; and this genius, in all its freshness, was
poured into the composition of *Faust*,—the most
kindred of themes, the most picturesque and magical of romances.

In Goethe's first version of the poem, before the
story of Gretchen, we find the studious Faust, as in
Marlowe, soliloquizing on the vanity of the sciences.
They grasp nothing of the genuine truth; they are
verbal shams. They have not even brought Faust

fame or riches. Perhaps magic might do better. The air was full of spirits; could they be summoned to our aid, possibly the secrets of nature might be unlocked. We might reach true science, and through it undreamt-of power over the material world. For Nature, according to Goethe, really has secrets. She is not all open to eventual inspection; she is no mere mechanism of minute parts and statable laws. Our last view of her, like our first glimpse, must be interpreted; from the sum of her manifestations we must divine her soul. Therefore only a poetic and rhetorical art, like magic, has any chance of unveiling her, and of bringing us face to face with the truth.

In this invocation of spirits, as Goethe's Faust makes it, there is no question of selling, or even of risking, the soul. This Faust, unlike Marlowe's, has no faith and no fear. From the point of view of the church he is damned already as an unbeliever; but, as an unbeliever, he is looking for salvation in another quarter. Like the bolder spirits of the Renaissance, he is hoping to find in universal nature, infinite, placid, non-censorious, an escape from the prison-house of Christian doctrine and Christian law. His magic arts are the sacrament that will initiate him into his new religion, the religion of nature. He turns to nature also in another sense, more characteristic of the age of Goethe than of that of Faust. He longs for grandiose solitudes. He feels that moon-

light, caves, mountains, driving clouds, would be his
best medicine and his best counsellors. The souls of
Rousseau, Byron, and Shelley are pre-incarnate in
this Faust, the epitome of all romantic rebellions.
They coexist there with the souls of Paracelsus and
Giordano Bruno. The wild aspects of nature, he
thinks, will melt and renew his heart, while magic
reveals the mysteries of cosmic law and helps him
to exploit them.

Full of these hopes, Faust opens his book of magic
at the sign of the Macrocosm: it shows him the mechanism of the world, all forces and events playing
into one another and forming an infinite chain. The
spectacle entrances him; he seems to have attained
one of his dearest ambitions. But here he comes at
once upon the other half, or, as Hegel would call it,
the other moment, of the romantic life. Every romantic ideal, once realized, disenchants. No matter
what we attain, our dissatisfaction must be perpetual.
Thus the vision of the universe, which Faust now
has before him, is, he remembers, only a vision; it is
a theory or conception.[1] It is not a rendering of the
inner life of the world as Shakespeare, for instance,
feels and renders it. Experience, as it comes to him
who lives and works, is not given by that theoretical

[1] *Faust*, Part i., *Studierzimmer*, i.:
      Welch Schauspiel! aber, ach! ein Schauspiel nur!
      Wo fass' ich dich, unendliche Natur?
      Euch, Brüste, wo?

vision; in science experience is turned into so many
reviewed events, the passage of so much substance
through so many forms. But Faust does not want an
image or description of reality; he yearns to enact
and to become the reality itself.

In this new search, he fixes his eye on the sign of
the Earth-Spirit, which seems more propitious to his
present wish. This sign is the key to all experience.
All experience tempts Faust; he shrinks from nothing that any mortal may have endured; he is ready
to undertake everything that any mortal may have
done. In all men he would live; and with the last man
he will be content to die.[1] So mighty is his yearn-
ing for experience that the Earth-Spirit is softened
and appears at his bidding. In a red flame he sees its
monstrous visage, and his enthusiasm is turned to
horror. Outspread before him is the furious, indis-
criminate cataract of life, the merciless flux, the infinite variety, the absolute inconstancy of it. This
general life is not for any individual to rehearse; it
bursts all bounds of personality. Each man may assimilate that part only which falls within his understanding, only that aspect which things wear from his

---

[1] *Faust*, Part i., *Studierzimmer:*

> Du, Geist der Erde, bist mir näher ;
> Schon fühl' ich meine Kräfte höher,
> Schon glüh' ich wie von neuem Wein ;
> Ich fühle Mut, mich in die Welt zu wagen,
> Der Erde Weh, der Erde Glück zu tragen, . . .
> Mit Stürmen mich herumzuschlagen
> Und in des Schiffbruchs Knirschen nicht zu zagen.

particular angle, and to his particular interests. *Du gleichst*, the Earth-Spirit cries to him, — *du gleichst dem Geist den du begreifst, nicht mir.*

This saying — that the life possible and good for man is the life of reason, not the life of nature — is a hard one to the romantic, unintellectual, insatiable Faust. He thinks, like many another philosopher of feeling, that since his is a part of the sum of experience, the whole of experience should be akin to his. But in fact the opposite is far nearer the truth. Man is constituted by his limitations, by his station contrasted with all other stations, and his purposes chosen from amongst all other purposes. Any great scope he can attain must be due to his powers of representation. His understanding may render him universal; his life never can. Faust, as he hears this sentence from the departing Earth-Spirit, collapses under it. He feels impotent to gainsay what the tumult of the world is thundering at him, but he will not accept on authority so unwelcome and chastening a truth. All his long experience to come will scarcely suffice to convince him of it.

These are the chief philosophical ideas that appear in the two earlier versions of Goethe's *Faust*, — the *Urfaust* and the *Fragment*. What Mephistopheles says to the young student is only a clever expansion of what Faust had said in his first monologue about the vanity of science and of the learned professions.

Mephistopheles, too, finds theory ashen, and the tree of life green and full of golden fruit; only, having more experience than Faust of the second disenchanting moment in the romantic dialectic, he foresees that this golden fruit also will turn to ashes in the mouth, as it did in the garden of Eden. Science is folly, but life is no better; for after all is not science a part of life?

When we turn to the first part in its final shape, or to the entire drama, we find many changes and additions that seem to transform the romantic picture of the opening scene, and to offer us a rounded philosophy. The changes, however, are more in expression than in ultimate substance, and the additions are chiefly new illustrations of the ancient theme. Critics who study the *Entstehungsgeschichte* of works of art help us to analyze them more intelligently and reproduce more accurately what, at various times, may have been the intention of their authors. Yet these bits of information would be dearly bought if we were distracted by them from what gives poetic value and individual character to the result—its total idiosyncrasy, its place in the moral world. The place in the moral world of Goethe's *Faust* as a whole is just the place which the opening scene gave it in the beginning. It fills more space, it touches more historical and poetic matters; but its centre is the old centre, and its result the old result. It remains romantic in its pictures and in its philosophy.

The first addition that promises to throw new light on the idea of the drama is the *Prologue in Heaven*. In imitation of *The Book of Job*, we find the morning stars—the three archangels—singing together; and then follows a very agreeable and humorous conversation between the Lord and Mephistopheles. The scene is in the style of mediaeval religious plays, and this circumstance might lead us to suppose that the point at issue was the salvation of Faust's soul. But that, in the literal sense, is far from being the case. As in *Job*, the question is what sentiments the tempted mortal will maintain during this life, not what fate will afterwards overtake his disembodied spirit. Dead men, Mephistopheles observes, do not interest him. He is not a devil from a subterranean hell, concerned, out of pique or ambition, to increase the population of tortured shades in that fabulous region. He dwells in the atmosphere of earth; he knows nothing of the suns or the worlds, —the life of man is his element.[1] He remains—what

---

[1] *Faust, Prolog im Himmel:*
                              Mit den Toten
        Hab' ich mich niemals gern befangen.
        Am meisten lieb' ich mir die vollen, frischen Wangen.
        Für einen Leichnam bin ich nicht zu Haus;
        Mir geht es, wie der Katze mit der Maus. . . .
        Von Sonn' und Welten weiss ich nichts zu sagen,
        Ich sehe nur, wie sich die Menschen plagen.

he was in the first versions of the play—a part of
the Earth-Spirit, one of its embodiments. His particular office, as we shall see presently, is to precipitate
that continual destruction which is involved in the
continual renewal of life. He finds it very foolish of
Faust to demand everything and be satisfied with
nothing; and his wager is that Faust may be brought
to demand nothing and be satisfied with what chance
throws in his way, that he shall lick the dust, and
lick it with pleasure,[1] that he shall renounce the
dignity of willing what is not and cannot be, and
crawl about, like the serpent, basking in the comforts
of the moment.

Against this, the Lord pronounces Faust to be
his servant,—the servant, that is, of an ideal,—and
declares that whoever strives after an ideal must
needs go astray; yet in his necessary errors, the good
man never misses the right road.[2] In other words,
to have an ideal to strive for, and, like Faust, never
to be satisfied, is itself the salvation of man. Faust
does not yet know this. He half believes there is
some concrete and ultimate good beyond, and so is
bitter and violent in his dissatisfaction; but in due

[1] *Faust, Prolog im Himmel:*
>   Staub soll er fressen, und mit Lust.

[2] Ibid.:
>   Es irrt der Mensch, so lang' er strebt.
>   Ein guter Mensch in seinem dunkeln Drange
>   Ist sich des rechten Weges wohl bewusst.

season he will come to clearness on this subject, and
understand that only he deserves freedom and life
who must daily win them afresh.[1] Mephistopheles
himself, with his mockeries and seductions, helps to
keep the world moving and men wide awake.[2] Imperfection is all that is possible in the world of action; but the angels may gather up and fix in thought
the perfect forms approached or suggested by existence.[3]

In the two earlier versions of *Faust*, Mephistopheles appears without introduction; we find him
amusing himself by giving ambiguous advice to an
innocent scholar, and accompanying Faust in his
wanderings. His mocking tone and miraculous powers mark him at once as the devil of the legend; but
several passages prove that he is a deputy of the
Earth-Spirit evoked by Faust in the beginning. That
he should be both devil and world-demon ought not

[1] *Faust*, Part II. Act v.:
> Ja! diesem Sinne bin ich ganz ergeben,
> Das ist der Weisheit letzter Schluss:
> Nur der verdient sich Freiheit wie das Leben,
> Der täglich sie erobern muss.

[2] Ibid., Part I., *Prolog im Himmel:*
> Des Menschen Thätigkeit kann allzu leicht erschlaffen,
> Er liebt sich bald die unbedingte Ruh;
> Drum geb' ich gern ihm den Gesellen zu,
> Der reizt und wirkt und muss als Teufel schaffen.

[3] Ibid.:
> Das Werdende, das ewig wirkt und lebt,
> Umfass' euch mit der Liebe holden Schranken,
> Und was in schwankender Erscheinung schwebt,
> Befestiget mit dauernden Gedanken!

to surprise the learned.[1] The devils of popular mediaeval religion were not cut out of whole cloth: they
were simply the Neoplatonic demons of the air, together with the gods of Olympus and the more ancient
chthonic deities, blackened by sectarian zeal, and de-
graded by a coarse and timid imagination. Many of
these pagan sprites, indeed, had been originally imp-
ish and mischievous, since not all the aspects of nature are lovely or propitious, nor all the dreams of
men. But as a whole they were without malice in
their irresponsible, elemental life,—winged powers
darting through space between the earth and the
moon. They were not dwellers in a subterranean
hell; they were not tormentors nor tormented.
Often they swarmed and sang blithely, as they do
in *Faust* and even in the *Wonder-working Magician;* and if at other times they croaked or hooted,
it was like frogs and owls, less lovely creatures than
humming-birds, but not less natural.

One of these less amiable spirits of the atmo-

[1] *Faust*, Part i., *Wald und Höhle:*

> Erhabner Geist, du gabst mir, gabst mir alles,
> Warum ich bat. Du hast mir nicht umsonst
> Dein Angesicht im Feuer zugewendet. . . .
>   O, dass dem Menschen nichts Vollkommnes wird,
> Empfind' ich nun. Du gabst zu dieser Wonne,
> Die mich den Göttern nah und näher bringt,
> Mir den Gefährten, &c.

Also, ibid., *Trüber Tag:* Grosser herrlicher Geist, der du mir zu erscheinen
würdigtest, der du mein Herz kennest und meine Seele, warum an den
Schandgesellen mich schmieden, der sich am Schaden weidet und am Ver-
derben sich letzt?

sphere, especially of its ambient fire, is the Mephistopheles of Goethe. Why he delighted in evil rather
than in good he himself explains in a profound and
ingenious fashion. Darkness or nothingness, he says,
existed alone before the birth of light. Nothingness
or darkness still remains the fundamental and, to
his mind, the better part of that mixture of being
and privation which we call existence. Nothing that
exists can be preserved, nor does it deserve to be;
therefore it would have been better if nothing had
ever existed.[1] To deny the value of whatever is, and
to wish to destroy it, according to him, is the only
rational ambition; he is the spirit that denies continually, he is the everlasting No. This spirit —
which we might compare with the Mars of Lucretius—has great power in the world; every change,
in one of its aspects, expresses it, since in one of its
aspects, every change is the destruction of something. This spirit is always willing evil, for it wills

[1] *Faust*, Part i., *Studierzimmer*, ii.:

> Ich bin der Geist, der stets verneint!
> Und das mit Recht; denn alles, was entsteht,
> Ist wert, dass es zu Grunde geht;
> Drum besser wär's, dass nichts entstünde. . . .
> Ich bin ein Teil des Teils, der anfangs alles war,
> Ein Teil der Finsternis, die sich das Licht gebar. . . .
> Was sich dem Nichts entgegenstellt,
> Das Etwas, diese plumpe Welt,
> So viel als ich schon unternommen,
> Ich wusste nicht ihr beizukommen. . . .
> Wie viele hab' ich schon begraben!
> Und immer cirkuliert ein neues, frisches Blut.
> So geht es fort, man möchte rasend werden!

death, with all the folly, crime, and despair that minister to death. But in willing evil, it is always accomplishing good; for these evils make for nothingness, and nothingness is the true good. The famous couplet—

Ein Teil von jener Kraft
Die stets das Böse will, und stets das Gute schafft—

is far from expressing the Hegelian commonplace with which it is usually identified. It does not mean that destruction serves a good purpose after all because it clears the way for "something higher." Mephistopheles is not one of those philosophers who think change and evolution a good in themselves. He does not admit that his activity, while aiming at evil, contributes unintentionally to the good. It contributes to the good intentionally, because the evil it does is, in his opinion, less than the evil it cures. He is the cruel surgeon to the disease of life.

If he admitted the other interpretation, he would be *ipso facto* converted to the view of the Lord in the *Prologue*. His naughtiness would become, in his own eyes, a needful service in the cause of life,—a condition of life being really vital and worth living. He might then continue his sly operations and biting witticisms, without one drop more of kindness, and yet be sanctioned in everything by the Absolute, and adopt the smile and halo of the optimist. He

would have perceived that he was the spice of life,
the yeast and red pepper of the world, necessary to
the perfect savour of the providential concoction.
As it is, Mephistopheles is far more modest. He
says that he wills evil, because what he wills is contrary to what his victims will; he is the great contra-
dictor, the blaster of young hopes. Yet he does good,
because these young hopes, if let alone, would lead
to misery and absurdity. His contradiction nips the
folly of living in the bud. To be sure, as he goes on
to acknowledge, the destructive power never wins a
decisive victory. While everything falls successively
beneath his sickle, the seeds of life are being scattered perpetually behind his back. The Lucretian
Venus has her innings, as well as the Lucretian Mars.
The eternal see-saw, the ancient flux, continues without end and without abatement.

Thus Mephistopheles has a philosophy, and is
justified and consistent in his own eyes; yet in the
course of the drama he wears various masks and has
various moods. All he says and does cannot be made
altogether compatible with the essence of his mind,
as Goethe finally conceived it. The dramatic figure of
Mephistopheles had been fixed long before in its
graphic characteristics. Mephistopheles, for instance,
is extremely old; he feels older than the universe.
There is nothing new for him; he has no illusions.
His feeling for anyone he sees is choked, as happens

to old people, by his feelings for the infinite number of persons he remembers. He is heartless, because he is impersonal and universal. He is altogether inhuman; he has not the shames nor the tastes of man. He often assumes the form of a dog,—it is his favourite mask in this earthly carnival. He is not averse to the witches' kitchen, with its senseless din and obscenity. He puts up good-naturedly with the grotesque etiquette of the spirit-world, observes all the rules about signing contracts in blood, knocking thrice, and respecting pentagrams. Why should he not? Dogs and demons of the air are forms of the Earth-Spirit as much as man; man has no special dignity that Mephistopheles should respect. Man's morality is one of the moralities, his conventions are not less absurd than the conventions of other monkeys. Mephistopheles has no prejudice against the snake; he understands and he despises his cousin, the snake, also. He understands and he despises himself; he has had time to know himself thoroughly.

His understanding, however, is not impartial, because he is the advocate of death; he cannot sympathize with the other half of the Earth-Spirit, which he does not represent,—the creative, propulsive, enamoured side, the side that worships the ideal, the love that makes the world go round. What enchants an ingenuous soul can only amuse Mephistopheles; what torments it gives him a sardonic satisfaction.

Thus he comes to be in fact a sour and mocking devil. At other times, when he opposes the silliness and romanticism of Faust, he seems to be the spokesman of all experience and reason; as when he warns Faust that to be at all you must be something in particular. Yet even this he says by way of checking and denying Faust's passion for the infinite. The soberest truth, when unwelcome, may seem to the sentimental as diabolical as the most cynical lie; so that in spite of the very unequal justness of his various sentiments, Mephistopheles retains his dramatic unity. We recognize his tone and, under whatever mask, we think him a villain and find him delightful.

Such is the spirit, and such are the conditions, in which Faust undertakes his adventures. He thirsts for all experience, including all experience of evil; he fears no hell; and he hopes for no happiness. He trusts in magic; that is, he believes, or is willing to make believe, that apart from any settled conditions laid down by nature or God, personal will can evoke the experience it covets by its sheer force and assurance. His bond with Mephistopheles is an expression of this romantic faith. It is no bargain to buy pleasures on earth at the cost of torments hereafter; for neither Goethe, nor Faust, nor Mephistopheles believes that such pleasures are worth having, or such torments possible.

The first taste Faust gets of the world is in Auerbach's cellar, and he finds it at once unpalatable. His mature and disdainful mind cannot be amused by the sodden merriment he sees there. He is without that simplicity and heartiness which might find even drunken gaiety attractive; to put up with such follies, one must know nothing, like Brander, or everything, like Mephistopheles. Faust still feels the "pathos of distance;" he is acutely conscious of something incomparably noble just out of reach. In the witches' kitchen, which he next visits, pleasure is still more ugly and shallow; here the din is even more nonsensical, and the fancy more obscene. Yet Faust comes forth with two points gained in his romantic rehabilitation; he has taken the elixir of youth and he has seen the image of Helen in a mirror. He is henceforth in love with ideal beauty, and being young again, he is able to find ideal beauty in the first woman he sees.

The great episode of Gretchen follows; and when he leaves her (after the duel with her brother) to view the wild revels of the Walpurgisnacht, his youth for a moment catches the contagion of that orgy. His love of ideal beauty, which remains unsatisfied, saves him, however, from any lasting illusion. He sees a little red mouse running out of the mouth of a nymph he is pursuing, and his momentary inclination turns to aversion. When he goes

back to Gretchen in her prison, it is too late for
him to do more than recognize the ruin he has
brought about,—Gretchen dishonoured, her mother
poisoned, her brother killed, her child drowned by
her in a pond, and she herself about to be executed.
Gretchen, who is the only true Christian in this
poem, refuses to be rescued, because she wishes to
offer her voluntary death in propitiation for her
grave, though almost involuntary, offences.

This is the end of Faust's career through the world
of private interests,—the little world,—and we may
well ask what has been the fruit of his experiments
so far. What strength or experience has he amassed
for his further adventures? The answer is to be found
in the first scene of the second part, where Goethe
reaches his highest potency as a poet and as a philosopher. We are transported to a remote, magnificent, virgin country. It is evening, and Faust is
lying, weary but restless, on a flowering hillside.
Kindly spirits of nature are hovering above his head.
Ariel, their leader, bids them bring solace to the
troubled hero. It is enough he was unfortunate—
they make no question whether he was a saint or a
sinner.[1] The spirits in chorus then sing four lovely

1 *Faust*, Part ii. Act i., *Anmutige Gegend:*
  Kleiner Elfen Geistergrösse
  Eilet, wo sie helfen kann ;
  Ob er heilig, ob er böse,
  Jammert sie der Unglücksmann.

stanzas, one for each watch of the night. The first
invokes peace, forgetfulness, surrender to the healing
influence of sleep. Pity and remorse, they seem to
say, in the words of Spinoza, are evil and vain ; fail-
ure is incidental ; error is innocent. Nature has no
memory; forgive yourself, and you are forgiven. The
song of the second watch merges the unhappy soul
again in the infinite incorruptible substance of nature. The stars, great or little, twinkling or pure, fill
the sky with their ordered peace, and the sea with
their trembling reflection. In this universal circulation there is no private will, no permanent division.
In the next watch we find the plastic stress of
nature beginning to reassert itself; seeds swell, sap
mounts up the thawing branches, buds grow full;
everything recovers a fresh individuality and a tender, untried will. Finally, the song of the fourth watch
bids the flowers open their petals and Faust his eyes.
Forces renewed in repose should tempt a new career.
Nature is open to the brave, to the intelligent; all
may be noble, who dare to be so.[1]

Soothed by these ministrations, Faust awakes full
of new strength and ambition. He watches with rapture the sunlight touch the mountain-tops and creep
down gradually into the valleys. When it reaches

[1] *Faust*, Part II. Act I., *Anmutige Gegend:*

> Alles kann der Edle leisten,
> Der versteht und rasch ergreift.

The whole scene will repay study.

him, he turns to look directly at the sun; but he is dazzled. He seems to remember the Earth-Spirit that had once allured and then rejected him. We wish, he says, to kindle our torch of life, and we produce a conflagration, a monstrous medley of joy and sorrow, love and hate. Let us turn our backs upon the sun, upon infinite force and infinite existence. Fitter for our eyes the waterfall over against it, the torrent of human affairs, broken into a myriad rills. Upon the mists that rise from it the sunlight paints a rainbow, always vanishing, but always restored. This is the true image of rational human achievement. We have our life in the iridescence of the world.[1] Or, as Shelley has said it for us,—

> *Life, like a dome of many-coloured glass,*
> *Stains the white radiance of eternity,*
> *Until death tramples it to fragments.*

This death, however, is itself unstable. The Lucretian Venus, by reshaping our senses and instincts, builds that coloured dome once more. The rainbow is renewed, as the mists rise again or the wind dies down, and creation is glorious as on the first day.

[1] *Faust*, Part ii. Act i., *Anmutige Gegend:*

> Des Lebens Fackel wollten wir entzünden,
> Ein Feuermeer umschlingt uns, welch ein Feuer! . . .
> So bleibe denn die Sonne mir im Rücken!
> Der Wassersturz, das Felsenriff durchbrausend,
> Ihn schau' ich an mit wachsendem Entzücken. . . .
> Allein wie herrlich, diesem Sturm erspriessend,
> Wölbt sich des bunten Bogens Wechseldauer, . . .
> Der spiegelt ab das menschliche Bestreben. . . .
> Am farbigen Abglanz haben wir das Leben.

This is Goethe's theory of rejuvenation and immortality. It is thoroughly naturalistic. There is a life after death, but only for such souls as have enough scope to identify themselves with those forms which nature, in her uncertain oscillations, always tends to reproduce. A deep mind has deep roots in nature,— it will bloom many times over. But what a deep mind carries over into its next incarnation—perhaps in some remote sphere—is not its conventional merits and demerits, its load of remorse, or its sordid memories. These are washed away in its new baptism. What remains is only what was deep in that deep mind, so deep that new situations may again imply and admit it.

When, after the scene with the Earth-Spirit, Faust thought of suicide, he regarded it as a means to escape from oppressive conditions and to begin a fresh life under conditions wholly different and unknown. It was as if a man in middle life, disgusted with his profession, should abandon it to take up another. Such a resolution is serious. It expresses a great dissatisfaction with things as they stand, but it also expresses a great hope. Death, for Faust, is an adventure, like any other; and if, contrary to his presumption, this adventure should prove the last, that, too, is a risk he is willing to run. Accordingly, as he lifted the poison to his lips, he drank to the dawn, to a new springtime of existence. It was by no means the saddest nor the weakest moment of his life.[1]

Although the sound of an Easter hymn checked him, bringing sentimental memories of a religion in which he no longer believed, the transformation scene he looked for was only postponed. There is not much difference between dying as he had thought to die and living as he was about to live. Venomous essences, artificially brewed, were hardly necessary to bring him to a new life; the adventures he was entering upon were suicidal enough, for he was to strive without hope of attainment, and to proceed by passionate wilfulness or magic, without accepting the discipline of art or reason. Now, at the close of the first part, he has drained this poisoned life to the dregs, and the fever into which he falls carries him of itself into a new existence. He is not grown better or more reasonable; he is simply starting afresh, like a new day or a new person. He retains, however, the fundamental part of his character; his will remains wayward, but indomitable, and his achievements remain fruitless. Only he will henceforth be romantic on a broader stage, that of history and civi-

---

[1] *Faust*, Part i., *Studierzimmer:*

> Ins hohe Meer werd' ich hinausgewiesen, . . .
> Zu neuen Sphären reiner Thätigkeit. . . .
> Hier ist es Zeit, durch Thaten zu beweisen,
> Dass Manneswürde nicht der Götterhöhe weicht, . . .
> Zu diesem Schritt sich heiter zu entschliessen
> Und wär' es mit Gefahr, ins Nichts dahin zu fliessen.

lization; and his magic will summon before him illusions somewhat more intellectual, counterfeits of beauty and of power. His old loves have blown over, like the storms of a bygone year; and with only a dreamlike memory of his past errors, he goes forth to meet a new day.

Among the allurements which, in the old legend, prompted Faust to sell his soul to the devil, one was the beauty of woman. The poor recluse, grown gray among his parchments, had never noticed real women, or had not found them beautiful. Pedantic child that he was, when he thought of the beauty of woman, he thought only of Helen of Troy. And Helen, to the Faust of the legend, was simply what Venus might be to Tannhäuser,—a woman more ravishing than other ravishing women. She was the supreme instance of a vulgar thing. The young Goethe, however, who was a poet and a true German, and loved with his soul, was not attracted by this ideal. He gave his Faust a tenderer love,—a love of the heart as well as of the senses. Later, also, when Goethe took up the old legend again in a more antiquarian spirit, and restored Helen to her place in it, he transformed her from a symbol of feminine beauty alone into a symbol for all beauty, and especially for the highest beauty, that of Hellas. The second love of Faust is the passion for classicism.

This passion in a romantic age is not so paradoxical as it may sound. Winckelmann and the philo-
logians were restoring something ancient. It was the
romantic passion for all experience—for the faded experience of the ancients also—that made, for them,
the poetry and the charm of antiquity. How dignified
everything was in those heroic days! How noble, serene, and abstracted! How pure the blind eyes of
statues, how chaste the white folds of the marble
drapery! Greece was a remote, fascinating vision, the
most romantic thing in the history of mankind. The
sad, delicious emotion one felt before a ruined temple
was as sentimental as anything one could feel before
a ruined castle, but more elegant and more choice.
It was sentimentality in marble. The heroes of the
Iliad were idealized in the same way as the savages
of Rousseau were idealized, or as the robbers of
Schiller.

The romantic classicism of the Napoleonic era lies
between the polite classicism of the French seventeenth century and the archaeological classicism of
our present Grecians. French classicism had been
quite indifferent to the picturesque aspects of ancient
life; it could tolerate on the stage an Achilles in a
periwig and laces. What the French tragedians had
adopted from the ancients was something inward, a
standard of character and motive, or a criterion of
taste. They studied harmony and restraint, not be-

cause these had been Greek qualities, but because
they were qualities essentially reasonable and beautiful, naturally belonging, even in modern times, to a
cultivated society and a cultivated poet. Again, the
admiration for Greece which is common in our
time among people of judgement differs from that of
Goethe and his age; for if we admire the artistic
expression of ancient life in poetry or sculpture, we
know that these manifestations were made possible
by a long political and moral discipline, and that, in
spite of that discipline, ancient art remained very
mixed, and often grotesque and impure.

For Goethe, however, as for Byron, Greece was
less a past civilization, to be studied scientifically,
than a living idea, a summons to new forms of art
and of sentiment. Goethe was never so romantic as
when he was classical. His distichs are like theatrical
gestures; he feels the sweep of his toga as he rounds
them off. His Iphigenia is a sentimental dream —
verflucht human, as he himself came to feel; and his
Helena is an evocation of magic, magical not merely
by accident and in the story, but essentially so, in
her ghostly semi-consciousness and glassy beauty.
The apparent incongruities of the scenes in which
she appears, surrounded by German knights in the
court of a feudal castle, are not real incongruities.
For this Helen is not a thing of the past; she is the
present dream and affectation of things classical in

a romantic era. Faust and his vassals offer Helen the most chivalrous and exaggerated homage; they introduce her, as a play queen, into their society. Faust retires with her to Arcadia,—the land of intentional and mid-summer idleness. Here a son, Euphorion, is born to them, a young genius, classic in aspect, but wildly romantic and ungovernable in temper. He scales the highest peaks, pursues by preference the nymphs that flee from him, loves violence and unreason, and finally, thinking to fly, falls headlong, like Icarus, and perishes. His last words call his mother after him, and she follows, leaving her veil and mantle behind, as Euphorion had left his lyre. On the mantle of Helen, which swells into a cloud, Faust is borne back again to his native Germany; its virtue, as he learns, is to lift him above all commonness.

This long allegory is charming enough, as a series of pictures and melodies, to leave the reader content not to interpret it; yet the intention of the poet is clear, if we care to disentangle it. By going down into the bowels of nature, where the earth goddesses dwell, who are the first mothers of all life and of all civilizations alike, we may gather intelligence to comprehend even the most alien existence. Greece, after such a reversion to the elemental, will appear to us in her unmatched simplicity and beauty. The vision will be granted us, although the object we see belongs to a distant past; and if our enthusiasm, like that of Faust, is passionate and indomitable, we may actually persuade the Queen of the Dead to yield up Helen that we may wed her. Our scholarship and philosophy, our faithful imitation of Greek art and literature, may actually render the Greek scene familiar to us. Yet the setting of this recovered genius will still be modern; it will become half modern itself; we shall have to teach Helen to rhyme. The product of this hybrid inspiration will be a romantic soul in the garb of classicism, a lovely wild thing, fated to die young. When this enthusiasm has dashed itself against the hard conditions of life, the beauty of Greece, that was its mother, will also pale before our eyes. We shall be, perforce, content to let it return to the realm of irrevocable past things. Only its garment, the monuments of its art and thought, will remain to raise us, if we have loved them, above all vulgarity in taste and in moral allegiance.

It is an evidence of Goethe's great wisdom that he felt that romantic classicism must be subordinated or abandoned; that Helen must evaporate, while Faust returned to Germany and to the feeling that after all Gretchen was his true love.[1] At the same time the issue of this wonderful episode is a little disappointing. At the beginning, the vision of Helen in a mirror had inspired Faust with renewed enthusiasm. The

---

[1] *Faust*, Part ii. Act iv., *Hochgebirg:* The first monologue.

sight of her again, in the magic play, had altogether
enraptured and overwhelmed him; and this inspiration had come just when, after the death of Gretchen,
he had resolved to pursue not all experience, as at
first, but rather the best experience,[1]—a hint that
the transformations of Faust's will were expected
somehow to constitute a real progress. There was,
indeed, among mortals such an infinite need of this
incomparable and symbolic Helen, that it could
move the very guardians of the dead to mercy and
to tears. When we remember all this, we have some
reason to expect that a great and permanent improvement in the life and heart of our hero should
follow on his obtaining so rare a boon. But to live
within Arcadia Helen was not needed; any Phyllis
would have served.

Helen, to be sure, leaves some relics behind, by
which we may understand that the influence of
Greek history, literature, and sculpture may still avail
to cultivate the mind and give it an air of distinction. Perhaps in the commonwealth he is about to
found, Faust would wish to establish not only dykes
and freedom, but also professorships of Greek and
archaeological museums. And the lyre of Euphorion,
which is also left us, may signify that poems like

---

[1] *Faust*, Part I. Act II., *Anmutige Gegend:*

    Du, Erde, . . . regst und rührst ein kräftiges Beschliessen
    Zum höchsten Dasein immerfort zu streben.

Byron's *Isles of Greece*, Keats's *Grecian Urn*, *Die Götter Griechenlands* of Schiller, and Goethe's own classical pieces will continue to enrich European literature. This is something, but not enough to lift Faust's immense enthusiasm for Helen above a crass illusion. That dream of a perfect beauty to be achieved, of a perfect life to be lived according to nature and reason, would have ended in a little scholarship and a little pedantry. Faust would have won Helen in order to hand her over to Wagner.

Helen was queen of Sparta; and although of course the Doric Sparta of Lycurgus was something much later, and had nothing to do with the Sparta of Homer, yet taken symbolically it is the happiest accident that Helen, the type of Greek perfection in beauty, should have been queen of Sparta, the type of Greek perfection in discipline. A Faust that had truly deserved and understood Helen would have built her an Hellenic city; he would have become himself an ἄναξ ἀνδρῶν, a master of men, one of those poets in things, those shapers of well-bred generations and wise laws, of which Plato speaks, contrasting them with Homer and other poets in words only. For the beauty of mind and body that fascinates the romantic classicist, and which inspired the ancient poets themselves, was not a product of idleness and sentimentality, nor of material and forced activity; it was a product of orderly war, religion, gymnastics, and deliberate self-government.

The next turn in Faust's fortunes actually finds him a trader, a statesman, an empire-builder; and if such a rolling stone could gather any moss, we should expect to see here, if anywhere, the fruits of that "aesthetic education of mankind" which Helen represented. We should expect Faust, who had lain in the lap of absolute beauty, to understand its nature. We should expect him, in eager search after perfection, to establish his state on the distinction between the better and the worse,—a distinction never to be abolished or obscured for one who has loved beauty. In other words, he might have established a moral society, founding it on great renunciations and on enlightened heroisms, so that the highest beauty might really come down and dwell within that city. But we find nothing of the sort. Faust founds his kingdom because he must do something; and his only ideal of what he hopes to secure for his subjects is that they shall always have something to do. Thus the will to live, in Faust, is not in the least educated by his experience. It changes its objects because it must; the passions of youth yield to those of age; and among all the illusions of his life the most fatuous is the illusion of progress.

It is characteristic of the absolute romantic spirit that when it has finished with something it must invent a new interest. It beats the bush for fresh game;

it is always on the verge of being utterly bored. So now that Helen is flown, Mephistopheles must come to the rescue, like an amiable nurse, and propose all sorts of pastimes. Frankfort, Leipzig, Paris, Versailles, are described, with the entertainments that life there might afford; but Faust, who was always *difficile*, has been rendered more so by his recent splendid adventures. However, a new impulse suddenly arises in his breast. From the mountain-top to which Helen's mantle has borne him, he can see the German Ocean, with its tides daily covering great stretches of the flat shore, and rendering them brackish and uninhabitable. It would be a fine thing to reclaim those wastes, to plant there a prosperous population. After Greece, Faust has a vision of Holland.

This last ambition of Faust's is as romantic as the others. He feels the prompting towards political art, as he had felt the prompting towards love or beauty.[1] The notion of transforming things by his will, of leaving for ages his mark upon nature and upon human society, fascinates him;[2] but this passion for

---

[1] *Faust*, Part II. Act IV., *Hochgebirg:*

> Erstaunenswürdiges soll geraten,
> Ich fühle Kraft zu kühnem Fleiss.
> Herrschaft gewinn' ich, Eigentum!
> Die That ist alles, nichts der Ruhm.
> Da wagt mein Geist, sich selbst zu überfliegen ;
> Hier möcht' ich kämpfen, dies möcht' ich besiegen.

[2] Ibid., Act V., *Grosser Vorhof des Palasts:*

> Es kann die Spur von meinen Erdetagen
> Nicht in Aeonen untergehn.

activity and power, which some simple-minded com-
mentators dignify with the name of altruism and of
living for others, has no steady purpose or standard
about it.[1] Goethe is especially lavish in details to
prove this point. Magic, the exercise of an unteach-
able will, is still Faust's instrument. Mephistopheles,
by various arts of illusion, secures the triumph of the
emperor in a desperate war which he is carrying on
against a justifiable insurrection. As a reward for the
aid rendered, Faust receives the shore marches in fief.
The necessary dykes and canals are built by magic;
the spirits that Mephistopheles commands dig and
build them with strange incantations. The commerce
that springs up is also illegitimate: piracy is involved
in it.

Nor is this all. On some sand-dunes that diversified
the original beach, an old man and his wife, Philemon and Baucis, lived before the advent of Faust
and his improvements. On the hillock, besides their
cottage, there stood a small chapel, with a bell which
disturbed Faust in his newly built palace, partly by
its importunate sound, partly by its Christian suggestions, and partly by reminding him that he was not
master of the country altogether, and that something

---

[1] *Faust,* Part II. Act IV., *Hochgebirg:*

Wer befehlen soll
Muss im Befehlen Seligkeit empfinden.
Ihm ist die Brust von hohem Willen voll,
Doch was er will, es darf's kein Mensch ergründen.

existed in it not the product of his magical will. The old people would not sell out; and in a fit of impatience Faust orders that they should be evicted by force, and transferred to a better dwelling elsewhere. Mephistopheles and his minions execute these orders somewhat roughly: the cottage and chapel are set on fire, and Philemon and Baucis are consumed in the flames, or buried in the ruins.

Faust regrets this accident; but it is one of those inevitable developments of action which a brave man must face, and forget as soon as possible. He had regretted in the same way the unhappiness of Gretchen, and, presumably, the death of Euphorion; but such is romantic life. His will, though shaken, is not extinguished by such misadventures. He would continue, if life could last, doing things that, in some respect, he would be obliged to regret: but he would banish that regret easily, in the pursuit of some new interest, and, on the whole, he would not regret having been obliged to regret them. Otherwise, he would not have shared the whole experience of mankind, but missed the important experience of self-accusation and of self-recovery.

It is impossible to suppose that the citizens he is establishing behind leaky dykes, so that they may always have something to keep them busy, would have given him unmixed satisfaction if he could really have foreseen their career in its concrete details. Holland is an interesting country, but hardly a spectacle which would long entrance an idealist like Faust, so exacting that he has found the arts and sciences wholly vain, domesticity impossible, and kitchens and beer-cellars beneath consideration. The career of Faust himself had been far more free and active than that of his industrious burghers could ever hope to be. His interest in establishing them is a masterful, irresponsible interest. It is one more arbitrary passion, one more selfish illusion. As he had no conscience in his love, and sought and secured nobody's happiness, so he has no conscience in his ambition and in his political architecture; but if only his will is done, he does not ask whether, judged by its fruits, it will be worth doing. As his immense dejection at the beginning, when he was a doctor in his laboratory, was not founded on any real misfortune, but on restlessness and a vague infinite ambition, so his ultimate satisfaction in his work is not founded on any good done, but on a passionate wilfulness. He calls the thing he wants for others good, because he now wants to bestow it on them, not because they naturally want it for themselves. Incapable of sympathy, he has a momentary pleasure in policy; and in the last and "highest" expression of his will, in his statesmanship and supposed public spirit, he remains romantic and, if need be, aggressive and criminal.

Meantime, his end is approaching. The smoke from that poor little conflagration turns into shadowy shapes of want, guilt, care, and death, which come and hover about him. Want is kept off by his wealth, and guilt is transcended by his romantic courage. But care slips through the keyhole, breathes upon him, and blinds him; while death, though he does not see it, follows close upon his heels. Nevertheless, the old man—Faust is in his hundredth year—is undaunted, and all his thoughts are intent on the future, on the work to which he has set his hand. He orders the digging to proceed on the canals he is building; but the spirits that seem to obey him are getting out of hand, and dig his grave instead.

When he feels death upon him, Faust has one of his most splendid moments of self-assertion. He has stormed through the world, he says, taking with equal thanks the buffets and rewards of fortune;[1] and the last word of wisdom he has learned is that no man deserves life or freedom who does not daily win them anew. He will leave the dykes he has thrown up against the sea to protect the nation he has established; a symbol that their health and freedom must consist in perpetual striving against an indomitable

---

[1] *Faust*, Part II. Act v., *Mitternacht:*

Ich bin nur durch die Welt gerannt:
Ein jed' Gelüst ergriff ich bei den Haaren,
Was nicht genügte, liess ich fahren,
Was mich entwischte, liess ich ziehn.

foe. The thought of many generations living in that
wholesome danger and labour fills him with satisfaction; he could almost say to this moment, in which
that prospect opens before his mind's eye, "Stay,
thou art so fair."[1] And with these words—a last
challenge and mock surrender to Mephistopheles—
he sinks into the grave open at his feet.

Who has won the wager? Faust has almost, though
not quite, pronounced the words which were to give
Mephistopheles the victory; but the sense of them
is new, and Mephistopheles has not succeeded in
making Faust surrender his will to will, his indefinite
idealism. Since what satisfies Faust is merely the
consciousness that this will to will is to be maintained, and that neither he, nor the colonists he has
brought into being, will ever lick the dust, and take
comfort, without any further aspiration, in the chance
pleasures of the moment. Faust has maintained his
enthusiasm for a stormy, difficult, and endless life.
He has been true to his romantic philosophy.

He is therefore saved, in the sense in which salvation is defined in the *Prologue in Heaven*, and presently again in the song of the angels that receive his
soul when they say: "Whosoever is unflagging in his

---

[1] *Faust*, Part ii. Act v., *Grosser Vorhof des Palasts:*

    Solch ein Gewimmel möcht ich sehn,
    Auf freiem Grund mit freiem Volke stehn.
    Zum Augenblicke dürft' ich sagen:
    Verweile doch, du bist so schön!

striving for ever, him we can redeem."[1] This salvation does not hang on any improvement in Faust's character,—he was sinful to the end, and had been God's unwitting servant from the very beginning,—nor does it lie in any revolution in his fortunes, as if in heaven he were to be differently employed than on earth. He is going to teach life to the souls of young boys, who have died too soon to have had in their own persons any experience of Rathskellers, Gretchens, Helens, and Walpurgisnachts.[2] Teaching (though not exactly in these subjects) had been Doctor Faustus' original profession; and the weariness of it was what had driven him to magic and almost to suicide, until he had escaped into the great world of adventure outside. Certainly, with his new pupils he will not be more content; his romantic restlessness will not forsake him in heaven. Some fine day he will throw his celestial school-books out of the window, and with his pupils after him, go forth to taste life in some windier region of the clouds.

No, Faust is not saved in the sense of being sanctified or brought to a final, eternal state of bliss. The only improvement in his nature has been that he has

[1] *Faust*, Part ii. Act v., *Himmel:*

> Wer immer strebend sich bemüht,
> Den können wir erlösen.

[2] Ibid. :

> Wir wurden früh entfernt
> Von Lebechören;
> Doch dieser hat gelernt,
> Er wird uns lehren.

passed, at the beginning of the second part, from private to public activities. If, at the end of this part, he expresses a wish to abandon magic and to live like a man among men, in the bosom of real nature, that wish remains merely Platonic.[1] It is a thought that visited Goethe often during his long career, that it is the part of wisdom to accept life under natural conditions rather than to pretend to evoke the conditions of life out of the will to live. This thought, were it held steadfastly, would constitute an advance from transcendentalism to naturalism. But the spirit of nature is itself romantic. It lives spontaneously, bravely, without premeditation, and for the sake of living rather than of enjoying or attaining anything final. And under natural conditions, the vicissitudes of an endless life would be many; and there could be no question of an ultimate goal, nor even of an endless progress in any particular direction. The veering of life is part of its vitality,—it is essential to romantic irony and to romantic pluck.

The secret of what is serious in the moral of *Faust* is to be looked for in Spinoza,—the source of what is serious in the philosophy of Goethe. Spinoza has an admirable doctrine, or rather insight, which he

---

[1] *Faust*, Part II. Act v., *Mitternacht:*

> Noch hab' ich mich ins Freie nicht gekämpft.
> Könnt ich Magie von meinem Pfad entfernen,
> Die Zaubersprüche ganz und gar verlernen,
> Stünd' ich, Natur, vor dir ein Mann allein,
> Da wär's der Mühe wert, ein Mensch zu sein.

calls seeing things under the form of eternity. This faculty is fundamental in the human mind; ordinary perception and memory are cases of it. Therefore, when we use it to deal with ultimate issues, we are not alienated from experience, but, on the contrary, endowed with experience and with its fruits. A thing is seen under the form of eternity when all its parts or stages are conceived in their true relations, and thereby conceived together. The complete biography of Caesar is Caesar seen under the form of eternity. Now the complete biography of Faust, Faust seen under the form of eternity, shows forth his salvation. God and Faust himself, in his last moment of insight, see that to have led such a life, in such a spirit, *was* to be saved; it was to be the sort of man a man should be. The blots on that life were helpful and necessary blots; the passions of it were necessary and creative passions. To have felt such perpetual dissatisfaction is truly satisfactory; such desire for universal experience is the right experience. You are saved in that you lived well; saved not after you have stopped living well, but during the whole process. Your destiny has been to be the servant of God. That God and your own conscience should pronounce this sentence is your true salvation. Your worthiness is thereby established under the form of eternity.

The play, in its philosophic development, ends here; but Goethe added several more details and

scenes, with that abundance, that love, of symbolic
pictures and poetic epigrams which characterizes the
whole second part. As Faust expires, or rather before he does so, Mephistopheles posts one of his little
demons at each aperture of the hero's body, lest the
soul should slip out without being caught. At the
same time a bevy of angels descends, scattering the
red roses of love and singing its praises. These roses,
if they touch Mephistopheles and his demons, turn
to balls of fire; and although fire is their familiar
element, they are scorched and scared away. The
angels are thus enabled to catch the soul of Faust
at their leisure, and bear it away triumphantly.

It goes without saying that this fight of little boys
over a fluttering butterfly cannot be what really determines the issue of the wager and the salvation of
Faust; but Goethe, in his conversations with Eckermann, justifies this intervention of a sort of mechanical accident, by the analogy of Christian doctrine. Grace is needed, besides virtue; and the intercession of Gretchen and the Virgin Mary, like that
of the Virgin Mary, Lucia, and Beatrice, in Dante's
case, and the stratagem of the balls of fire, all stand
for this external condition of salvation.

This intervention of grace is, at bottom, only a
new symbol for the essential justification, under the
form of eternity, of what is imperfect and insufficient
in time. The chequered and wilful life of Faust is

not righteous in any of its parts; yet righteousness is imputed to it as a whole; divine love accepts it as sufficient; speculative reason declares that to be the best possible life which, to humdrum understanding, seems a series of faults and of failures. If the foretaste of his new Holland fills, from a distance, the dying Faust with satisfaction, how much more must the wonderful career of Faust himself deserve to be accepted and envied, and proclaimed to be its own excuse for being! The faults of Faust in time are not counted against him in eternity. His crimes and follies were blessings in disguise. Did they not render his life interesting and fit to make a poem of? Was it not by falling into them, and rising out of them, that Faust was Faust at all? This insight is the higher reason, the divine love, supervening to save him. What ought to be imperfect in time is, because of its very imperfection there, perfect when viewed under the form of eternity. To live, to live just as we do, that—if we could only realize it—is the purpose and the crown of living. We must seek improvement; we must be dissatisfied with ourselves; that is the appointed attitude, the histrionic pose, that is to keep the ball rolling. But while we feel this dissatisfaction we are perfectly satisfactory, and while we play our game and constantly lose it, we are winning the game for God.

Even this scene, however, did not satisfy the pro-

lific fancy of the poet, and he added a final one,
—the apotheosis or *Himmelfahrt* of Faust. In the
Campo Santo at Pisa Goethe had seen a fresco representing various anchorites dwelling on the flanks
of some sacred mountain,— Sinai, Carmel, or Athos,
—each in his little cave or hermitage; and above
them, in the large space of sky, flights of angels were
seen rising towards the Madonna. Through such a
landscape the poet now shows us the soul of Faust
carried slowly upwards.

This scene has been regarded as inspired by Catholic ideas, whereas the *Prologue in Heaven* was Biblical and Protestant; and Goethe himself says that
his "poetic intention" could best be rendered by images borrowed from the tradition of the mediaeval
church. But in truth there is nothing Catholic about
the scene, except the names or titles of the personages. What they say is all sentimental landscape-
painting or vague mysticism, such as might go with
any somewhat nebulous piety; and much is actually
borrowed from Swedenborg. What is Swedenbor-
gian, however,—such as the notion of heavenly in-
struction, passage from sphere to sphere, and looking
through other people's eyes,—is in turn a mere form
of expression. The "poetic intention" of the author is,
as we have seen, altogether Spinozitic. Undoubtedly
he conceives that the soul of Faust is to pass, in another world, through some new series of experiences.

But that destiny is not his salvation; it is the continuance of his trial. The famous chorus at the very
end repeats, with an interesting variation, the same
contrast we have seen before between the point of
view of time and that of eternity. Everything transitory, says the mystic chorus,[1] is only an image;
here (that is, under the form of eternity) the insufficient is turned into something actual and complete;
and what seemed in experience an endless pursuit
becomes to speculation a perfect fulfilment. The ideal
of something infinitely attractive and essentially inexhaustible—the eternal feminine, as Goethe calls
it — draws life on from stage to stage.

Gretchen and Helen had been symbols of this
ideal; Goethe's green old age had felt, to the very
last, the charm of woman, the sweetness and the
sorrow of loving what he could not hope to possess,
and what, in its ideal perfection, necessarily eludes
possession. He had reconciled himself, not without
tears, to this desire without hope, and, like Piccarda
in the *Paradiso*, he had blessed the hand that gave the

---

[1] *Faust*, Part II. Act v., *Himmel*:

> Alles Vergängliche
> Ist nur ein Gleichnis ;
> Das Unzulängliche,
> Hier wird's Ereignis;
> Das Unbeschreibliche,
> Hier ist es gethan ;
> Das Ewig-Weibliche
> Zieht uns hinan.

passion and denied the happiness.[1] Thus, in dreaming
of one satisfaction and renouncing it, he had found
a satisfaction of another kind. *Faust* ends on the
same philosophical level on which it began,—the
level of romanticism. The worth of life lies in pursuit, not in attainment; therefore, everything is worth
pursuing, and nothing brings satisfaction—save this
endless destiny itself.

Such is the official moral of *Faust*, and what we
may call its general philosophy. But, as we saw just
now, this moral is only an afterthought, and is far
from exhausting the philosophic ideas which the
poem contains. Here is a scheme for experience; but
experience, in filling it out, opens up many vistas;
and some of these reveal deeper and higher things
than experience itself. The path of the pilgrim and
the inns he stops at are neither the whole landscape
he sees as he travels, nor the true shrine he is making for. And the incidental philosophy or philosophies of Goethe's *Faust* are, to my mind, often better than its ultimate philosophy. The first scene of
the second part, for instance, is better, poetically
and philosophically, than the last. It shows a deeper

[1] Cf. *Trilogie der Leidenschaft*, 1823 :

>   Mich treibt umher ein unbezwinglich Sehnen ;
>   Da bleibt kein Rat als grenzenlose Thränen. . . .
>   Und so das Herz erleichtert merkt behende
>   Dass es noch lebt und schlägt und möchte schlagen, . . .
>   Da fühlte sich—o, dass es ewig bliebe!—
>   Das Doppelglück der Töne wie der Liebe.

sense for the realities of nature and of the soul, and it is more sincere. Goethe there is interpreting nature with Spinoza; he is not dreaming with Swedenborg, nor talking equivocal paradoxes with Hegel.

In fact, the great merit of the romantic attitude in poetry, and of the transcendental method in philosophy, is that they put us back at the beginning of our experience. They disintegrate convention, which is often cumbrous and confused, and restore us to ourselves, to immediate perception and primordial will. That, as it would seem, is the true and inevitable starting-point. Had we not been born, had we not peeped into this world, each out of his personal eggshell, this world might indeed have existed without us, as a thousand undiscoverable worlds may now exist; but for us it would not have existed. This obvious truth would not need to be insisted on but for two reasons: one that conventional knowledge, such as our notions of science and morality afford, is often top-heavy; asserts and imposes on us much more than our experience warrants,—our experience, which is our only approach to reality. The other reason is the reverse or counterpart of this; for conventional knowledge often ignores and seems to suppress parts of experience no less actual and important for us as those parts on which the conventional knowledge itself is reared. The public world is too narrow for the soul, as well as too mythical and fabulous. Hence the double critical labour and reawakening which romantic reflection is good for,—to cut off the dead branches and feed the starving shoots. This philosophy, as Kant said, is a cathartic: it is purgative and liberating; it is intended to make us start afresh and start right.

It follows that one who has no sympathy with such a philosophy is a comparatively conventional person. He has a second-hand mind. Faust has a first-hand mind, a truly free, sincere, courageous soul. It follows also, however, that one who has no philosophy but this has no wisdom; he can say nothing that is worth carrying away; everything in him is attitude and nothing is achievement. Faust, and especially Mephistopheles, do have other philosophies on top of their transcendentalism; for this is only a method, to be used in reaching conclusions that shall be critically safeguarded and empirically grounded. Such outlooks, such vistas into nature, are scattered liberally through the pages of *Faust*. Words of wisdom diversify this career of folly, as exquisite scenes fill this tortuous and overloaded drama. The mind has become free and sincere, but it has remained bewildered.

The literary merits of Goethe's *Faust* correspond accurately with its philosophical excellences. In the prologue in the theatre Goethe himself has described them; much scenery, much wisdom, some folly, great wealth of incident and characterization; and behind, the soul of a poet singing with all sincerity and fervour the visions of his life. Here is profundity, inwardness, honesty, waywardness; here are the most touching accents of nature, and the most varied assortment of curious lore and grotesque fancies. This work, says Goethe (in a quatrain intended as an epilogue, but not ultimately inserted in the play),— this work is like human life: it has a beginning, it has an end; but it has no totality, it is not one whole.[1] How, indeed, should we draw the sum of an infinite experience that is without conditions to determine it, and without goals in which it terminates? Evidently all a poet of pure experience can do is to represent some snatches of it, more or less prolonged; and the more prolonged the experience represented is the more it will be a collection of snatches, and the less the last part of it will have to do with the beginning. Any character which we may attribute to the whole of what we have surveyed would fail to dominate it, if that whole had been larger, and if we had had memory or foresight enough to include other parts of experience differing altogether in kind from the episodes we happen to have lived through. To be miscellaneous, to be indefinite, to be unfinished,

---

[1] *Aus dem Nachlass, Abkündigung:*

> Des Menschen Leben ist ein ähnliches Gedicht;
> Es hat wohl einen Anfang, hat ein Ende,
> Allein ein Ganzes ist es nicht.

is essential to the romantic life. May we not say that
it is essential to all life, in its immediacy; and that
only in reference to what is not life—to objects,
ideals, and unanimities that cannot be experienced
but may only be conceived—can life become rational
and truly progressive? Herein we may see the radical and inalienable excellence of romanticism; its
sincerity, freedom, richness, and infinity. Herein, too,
we may see its limitations, in that it cannot fix or
trust any of its ideals, and blindly believes the universe to be as wayward as itself, so that nature and
art are always slipping through its fingers. It is ob-
stinately empirical, and will never learn anything
from experience.

CONCLUSION

V
CONCLUSION

IT may be possible, after studying these three philosophical poets, to establish some comparison
between them. By a comparison is not meant a
discussion as to which of our poets is the best. Each
is the best in his way, and none is the best in every
way. To express a preference is not so much a criticism as a personal confession. If it were a question
of the relative pleasure a man might get from each
poet in turn, this pleasure would differ according to
the man's temperament, his period of life, the language he knew best, and the doctrine that was most
familiar to him. By a comparison is meant a review
of the analysis we have already made of the type of
imagination and philosophy embodied in each of the
poets, to see what they have in common, how they
differ, or what order they will fall into from different
points of view. Thus we have just seen that Goethe,
in his *Faust*, presents experience in its immediacy,
variety, and apparent groundlessness; and that he
presents it as an episode, before and after which other
episodes, differing from it more and more as you recede, may be conceived to come. There is no possible totality in this, for there is no known ground.
Turn to Lucretius, and the difference is striking. Lucretius is the poet of substance. The ground is what

he sees everywhere; and by seeing the ground, he sees also the possible products of it. Experience appears in Lucretius, not as each man comes upon it in his own person, but as the scientific observer views it from without. Experience for him is a natural, inevitable, monotonous round of feelings, involved in the operations of nature. The ground and the limits of experience have become evident together.

In Dante, on the other hand, we have a view of experience also in its totality, also from above and, in a sense, from outside ; but the external point of reference is moral, not physical, and what interests the poet is what experience is best, what processes lead to a supreme, self-justifying, indestructible sort of existence. Goethe is the poet of life; Lucretius the poet of nature; Dante the poet of salvation. Goethe gives us what is most fundamental,—the turbid flux of sense, the cry of the heart, the first tentative notions of art and science, which magic or shrewdness might hit upon. Lucretius carries us one step farther. Our wisdom ceases to be impressionistic and casual. It rests on understanding of things, so that what happiness remains to us does not deceive us, and we can possess it in dignity and peace. Knowledge of what is possible is the beginning of happiness. Dante, however, carries us much farther than that. He, too, has knowledge of what is possible and impossible. He has collected the precepts of old philosophers and saints, and the more recent examples patent in society around him, and by their help has distinguished the ambitions that may be wisely indulged in this life from those which it is madness to foster,—the first being called virtue and piety and the second folly and sin. What makes such knowledge precious is not only that it sketches in general the scope and issue of life, but that it paints in the detail as well,—the detail of what is possible no less than that (more familiar to tragic poets) of what is impossible.

Lucretius' notion, for instance, of what is positively worth while or attainable is very meagre: freedom from superstition, with so much natural science as may secure that freedom, friendship, and a few cheap and healthful animal pleasures. No love, no patriotism, no enterprise, no religion. So, too, in what is forbidden us, Lucretius sees only generalities,—the folly of passion, the blight of superstition. Dante, on the contrary, sees the various pitfalls of life with intense distinctness; and seeing them clearly, and how fatal each is, he sees also why men fall into them, the dream that leads men astray, and the sweetness of those goods that are impossible. Feeling, even in what we must ultimately call evil, the soul of good that attracts us to it, he feels in good all its loveliness and variety. Where, except in Dante, can we find so many stars that differ from other stars in glory;

so many delightful habitations for excellences; so many distinct beauties of form, accent, thought, and intention; so many delicacies and heroisms? Dante is the master of those who know by experience what is worth knowing by experience; he is the master of *distinction*.

Here, then, are our three poets and their messages: Goethe, with human life in its immediacy, treated romantically; Lucretius, with a vision of nature and of the limits of human life; Dante, with spiritual mastery of that life, and a perfect knowledge of good and evil.

You may stop at what stage you will, according to your sense of what is real and important; for what one man calls higher another man calls unreal; and what one man feels to be strength smells rank to another. In the end, we should not be satisfied with any one of our poets if we had to drop the other two. It is true that taken formally, and in respect to their type of philosophy and imagination, Dante is on a higher plane than Lucretius, and Lucretius on a higher plane than Goethe. But the plane on which a poet dwells is not everything; much depends on what he brings up with him to that level. Now there is a great deal, a very great deal, in Goethe that Lucretius does not know of. Not knowing of it, Lucretius cannot carry this fund of experience up to the intellectual and naturalistic level; he cannot transmute this abundant substance of Goethe's by his higher insight and clearer faith; he has not woven so much into his poem. So that while to see nature, as Lucretius sees it, is a greater feat than merely to live hard in a romantic fashion, and produces a purer and more exalted poem than Goethe's magical medley, yet this medley is full of images, passions, memories, and introspective wisdom that Lucretius could not have dreamed of. The intellect of Lucretius rises, but rises comparatively empty; his vision sees things as a whole, and in their right places, but sees very little of them; he is quite deaf to their intricacy, to their birdlike multiform little souls. These Goethe knows admirably; with these he makes a natural concert, all the more natural for being sometimes discordant, sometimes overloaded and dull. It is necessary to revert from Lucretius to Goethe to get at the volume of life.

So, too, if we rise from Lucretius to Dante, there is much left behind which we cannot afford to lose. Dante may seem at first sight to have a view of nature not less complete and clear than that of Lucretius; a view even more efficacious than materialism for fixing the limits of human destiny and marking the path to happiness. But there is an illusion here. Dante's idea of nature is not genuine; it is not sincerely put together out of reasoned observation. It is a view of nature intercepted by myths and worked out by dialectic. Consequently, he has no true idea either of the path to happiness or of its real conditions. His notion of nature is an inverted image of the moral world, cast like a gigantic shadow upon the sky. It is a mirage.

Now, while to know evil, and especially good, in all their forms and inward implications is a far greater thing than to know the natural conditions of good and evil, or their real distribution in space and time, yet the higher philosophy is not safe if the lower philosophy is wanting or is false. Of course it is not safe practically; but it is not safe even poetically. There is an attenuated texture and imagery in the *Divine Comedy*. The voice that sings it, from beginning to end, is a thin boy-treble, all wonder and naïveté. This art does not smack of life, but of somnambulism. The reason is that the intellect has been hypnotized by a legendary and verbal philosophy. It has been unmanned, curiously enough, by an excess of humanism; by the fond delusion that man and his moral nature are at the centre of the universe. Dante is always thinking of the divine order of history and of the spheres; he believes in controlling and chastening the individual soul; so that he seems to be a cosmic poet, and to have escaped the anthropocentric conceit of romanticism. But he has not escaped it. For, as we have seen, this golden cage in which his soul sings is artificial; it is constructed on purpose to satisfy and glorify human distinctions and human preferences. The bird is not in his native wilds; man is not in the bosom of nature. He is, in a moral sense, still at the centre of the universe; his ideal is the cause of everything. He is the appointed lord of the earth, the darling of heaven; and history is a brief and prearranged drama, with Judea and Rome for its chief theatre.

Some of these illusions are already abandoned; all are undermined. Sometimes, in moments when we are unnerved and uninspired, we may regret the ease with which Dante could reconcile himself to a world, so imagined as to suit human fancy, and flatter human will. We may envy Dante his ignorance of nature, which enabled him to suppose that he dominated it, as an infinite and exuberant nature cannot be dominated by any of its parts. In the end, however, knowledge is good for the imagination. Dante himself thought so; and his work proved that he was right, by infinitely excelling that of all ignorant contemporary poets. The illusion of knowledge is better than ignorance for a poet; but the reality of knowledge would be better than the illusion; it would stretch the mind over a vaster and more stimulating scene; it would concentrate the will upon a more attainable, distinct, and congenial happiness. The growth of what is known increases the scope of what may be imagined and hoped for.

Throw open to the young poet the infinity of nature; let him feel the precariousness of life, the variety of purposes, civilizations, and religions even upon this little planet; let him trace the triumphs and follies of art and philosophy, and their perpetual resurrections — like that of the downcast Faust. If, under the stimulus of such a scene, he does not some day compose a natural comedy as much surpassing Dante's divine comedy in sublimity and richness as it will surpass it in truth, the fault will not lie with the subject, which is inviting and magnificent, but with the halting genius that cannot render that subject worthily.

Undoubtedly, the universe so displayed would not be without its dark shadows and its perpetual tragedies. That is in the nature of things. Dante's cosmos, for all its mythical idealism, was not so false as not to have a hell in it. Those rolling spheres, with all their lights and music, circled for ever about hell. Perhaps in the real life of nature evil may not prove to be so central as that. It would seem to be rather a sort of inevitable but incidental friction, capable of being diminished indefinitely, as the world is better known and the will is better educated. In Dante's spheres there could be no discord whatever; but at the core of them was eternal woe. In the star-dust of our physics discords are everywhere, and harmony is only tentative and approximate, as it is in the best earthly life; but at the core there is nothing sinister, only freedom, innocence, inexhaustible possibilities of all sorts of happiness. These possibilities may tempt future poets to describe them; but meantime, if we wish to have a vision of nature not fundamentally false, we must revert from Dante to Lucretius.

Obviously, what would be desirable, what would constitute a truly philosophical or comprehensive poet, would be the union of the insights and gifts which our three poets have possessed. This union is not impossible. The insights may be superposed one on the other. Experience in all its extent, what Goethe represents, should be at the foundation. But as the extent of experience is potentially infinite, as there are all sorts of worlds possible and all sorts of senses and habits of thought, the widest survey would still leave the poet, where Goethe leaves us, with a sense of an infinity beyond. He would be at liberty to summon from the limbo of potentiality any form that interested him; poetry and art would recover their early freedom; there would be no beauties forbidden and none prescribed. For it is a very liberating and sublime thing to summon up, like Faust, the image of *all* experience. Unless that has been done, we leave the enemy in our rear; whatever interpretations we offer for experience will become impertinent and worthless if the experience we work upon is no longer at hand. Nor will any construction, however broadly based, have an *absolute* authority; the indomitable freedom of life to be more, to be new, to be what it has not entered into the heart of man as yet to conceive, must always remain standing. With that freedom goes the modesty of reason, both in physics and in morals, that can lay claim only to partial knowledge, and to the ordering of a particular soul, or city, or civilization.

Poetry and philosophy, however, are civilized arts; they are proper to some particular genius, which has succeeded in flowering at a particular time and place. A poet who merely swam out into the sea of sensibility, and tried to picture all possible things, real or unreal, human or inhuman, would bring materials only to the workshop of art; he would not be an artist. To the genius of Goethe he must add that of Lucretius and Dante.

There are two directions in which it seems fitting that rational art should proceed, on the basis which a limited experience can give it. Art may come to buttress a particular form of life, or it may come to express it. All that we call industry, science, business, morality, buttresses our life; it informs us about our conditions and adjusts us to them; it equips us for life; it lays out the ground for the game we are to play. This preliminary labour, however, need not be servile. To do it is also to exercise our faculties;

and in that exercise our faculties may grow free,—
as the imagination of Lucretius, in tracing the course
of the atoms, dances and soars most congenially.
One extension of art, then, would be in the direction of doing artistically, joyfully, sympathetically,
whatever we have to do. Literature in particular
(which is involved in history, politics, science, affairs)
might be throughout a work of art. It would become so not by being ornate, but by being appropriate; and the sense of a great precision and justness
would come over us as we read or wrote. It would
delight us; it would make us see how beautiful, how
satisfying, is the art of being observant, economi-
cal, and sincere. The philosophical or comprehensive
poet, like Homer, like Shakespeare, would be a poet
of business. He would have a taste for the world in
which he lived, and a clean view of it.

There remains a second form of rational art, that
of expressing the ideal towards which we would move
under these improved conditions. For as we react we
manifest an inward principle, expressed in that re-
action. We have a nature that selects its own direction, and the direction in which practical arts shall
transform the world. The outer life is for the sake of
the inner; discipline is for the sake of freedom, and
conquest for the sake of self-possession. This inner
life is wonderfully redundant; there is, namely, very
much more in it than a consciousness of those acts

by which the body adjusts itself to its surroundings. *Am farbigen Abglanz haben wir das Leben;* each sense has its arbitrary quality, each language its arbitrary euphony and prosody; every game has its creative laws, every soul its own tender reverberations and secret dreams. Life has a margin of play which might grow broader, if the sustaining nucleus were more firmly established in the world. To the art of working well a civilized race would add the art of playing well. To play with nature and make it decorative, to play with the overtones of life and make them delightful, is a sort of art. It is the ultimate, the most artistic sort of art, but it will never be practised successfully so long as the other sort of art is in a backward state; for if we do not know our environment, we shall mistake our dreams for a part of it, and so spoil our science by making it fantastic, and our dreams by making them obligatory. The art and the religion of the past, as we see conspicuously in Dante, have fallen into this error. To correct it would be to establish a new religion and a new art, based on moral liberty and on moral courage.

Who shall be the poet of this double insight? He has never existed, but he is needed nevertheless. It is time some genius should appear to reconstitute the shattered picture of the world. He should live in the continual presence of all experience, and respect it; he should at the same time understand nature, the ground of that experience; and he should also have a delicate sense for the ideal echoes of his own passions, and for all the colours of his possible happiness. All that can inspire a poet is contained in this task, and nothing less than this task would exhaust a poet's inspiration. We may hail this needed genius from afar. Like the poets in Dante's limbo, when Virgil returns among them, we may salute him, saying: *Onorate l'altissimo poeta*. Honour the most high poet, honour the highest possible poet. But this supreme poet is in limbo still.

COLLEGE OF MARIN

3 2555 00111462 3

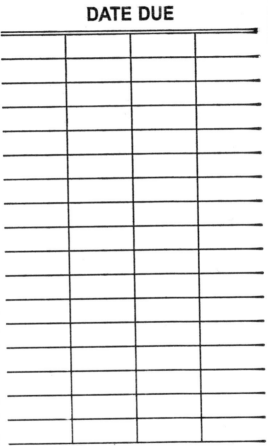

DATE DUE

Demco, Inc. 38-293